SIDE by SIDE

ACTIVITY WORKBOOK

Second Edition

2

Steven J. Molinsky

Bill Bliss

with

Carolyn Graham

Contributing Authors

Elizabeth Handley / *Katharine Kolowich* / with *Mary Ann Perry*

Longman

Editorial/production supervision: Janet Johnston
Art supervision: Karen Salzbach
Manufacturing buyer: Peter Havens
Cover design: Kenny Beck

Illustrated by Richard E. Hill

© 1989 by Prentice Hall Regents
A Pearson Education Company
Pearson Education
10 Bank Street, White Plains, NY 10606

Printed in the United States of America

20   19

ISBN 0-13-811746-2

CONTENTS

1 Like to
Review of Tenses:
  Simple Present
  Simple Past
  Future: Going to
Time Expressions
Indirect Object Pronouns   1

2 Count/Non-Count Nouns   11

3 Partitives
Count/Non-Count Nouns
Imperatives   22

4 Future Tense: Will
Time Expressions
Might   32

5 Comparatives
Should
Possessive Pronouns   41

6 Superlatives   54

7 Directions   64

8 Adverbs
Comparative of Adverbs
Agent Nouns
If-Clauses   72

9 Past Continuous Tense
Reflexive Pronouns
While-Clauses   84

10 Could
Be Able to
Have Got to
Too + Adjective   93

11 Must
Must vs. Should
Count/Non-Count Nouns
Past Tense Review   103

12 Future Continuous Tense
Time Expressions   111

13 Some/Any
Pronoun Review
Verb Tense Review   120

Tape Scripts for Listening Exercises   133

Correlation Key   136

A. LIKES AND DISLIKES

bake	eat	study	visit	watch
dance	play	teach	wait for	write to

like to
likes to

don't like to
doesn't like to

1. Alan _____likes to play_____ chess.

2. Mrs. Johnson _____doesn't like_____
_____to teach_____.

3. Ted and Patty _____
ice cream.

4. Mr. and Mrs. Taylor _____
_____.

5. Susan _____ her
grandparents.

6. David _____
_____.

7. We _____ TV together.

8. I _____.

9. Mary _____ her
friends.

10. Mr. Jackson _____
_____ the train.

B. RHYTHM AND RHYME: *She Likes to Ride*

Listen. Then clap and practice.

She likes to ride.
He likes to walk.
She likes to listen.
He likes to talk.

They like to swim.
We like to sail.
I like to open
the morning mail.

He likes to read.
She likes to write.
I like to stay up
late at night.

C. RHYTHM AND RHYME: *I Don't Like to Rush*

Listen. Then clap and practice.

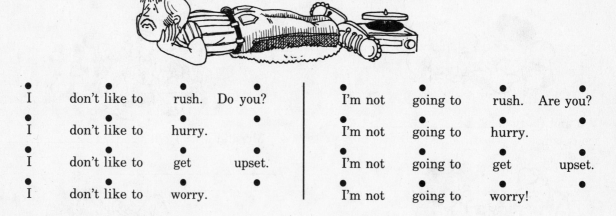

I don't like to rush. Do you?
I don't like to hurry.
I don't like to get upset.
I don't like to worry.

I'm not going to rush. Are you?
I'm not going to hurry.
I'm not going to get upset.
I'm not going to worry!

D. RHYTHM AND RHYME: *He Doesn't Like to Watch TV*

Listen. Then clap and practice.

He doesn't like to watch TV.
He doesn't like to dance.
He doesn't like to cook or sew
or wash or iron his pants.

She doesn't like to go to the beach.
She doesn't like to shop.
She doesn't like to vacuum her rugs
or dust or wax or mop.

2

E. WRITE ABOUT YOURSELF

What do you like to do?

1. I like to ....

2. ....

3. ....

4. ....

5. ....

What don't you like to do?

1. I don't like to ....

2. ....

3. ....

4. ....

5. ....

F. DAY AFTER DAY

brush	clean	do	go	read	take	wash
buy	cry	get up	have	sing	talk	write

1. Tommy ___*talks*___ to his girlfriend every evening.

   Yesterday evening he ___*talked to his girlfriend*___ .

   Tomorrow evening ___*he's going to talk to his girlfriend*___ .

2. Bobby and Billy _____ their bedroom every Saturday.

   Last Saturday they _____ .

   Next Saturday _____ .

3. Mr. Nelson _____ his car every Sunday.

   Last Sunday he _____ .

   Next Sunday _____ .

4. I _____ to my son every week.

   Last week I _____ .

   Next week _____ .

(continued)

5. We _____ together every Sunday.

Last Sunday we _____

_____ .

Next Sunday _____

_____ .

6. Our baby _____ every night.

Last night she _____

_____ .

Tomorrow night _____

_____ .

7. My children _____ dessert
every evening.

Yesterday evening they _____

_____ .

Tomorrow evening _____

_____ .

8. I _____ at 8:00 every morning.

Yesterday morning I _____

_____ .

Tomorrow morning _____

_____ .

9. Mrs. Green _____ the newspaper
every morning.

Yesterday morning she _____

_____ .

Tomorrow morning _____

_____ .

10. My mother and father _____ to the
movies every Saturday.

Last Saturday they _____

_____ .

Next Saturday _____

_____ .

11. Robert _____ bananas every week.

Last week he _____

_____ .

Next week _____

_____ .

12. Our children _____ their teeth every morning.

Yesterday morning they _____

_____ .

Tomorrow morning _____

_____ .

13. Anna _____ the bus every morning.

Yesterday morning she _____

_____ .

Tomorrow morning _____

_____ .

14. My brother and I _____ our exercises every afternoon.

Yesterday afternoon we _____

_____ .

Tomorrow afternoon _____

_____ .

15. I .... every ....

Yesterday/Last .... I ....

Tomorrow/Next ....

5

G. RHYTHM: *I'm Not Going to Call Him Again*

Listen. Then clap and practice.

A.   Are you going to call   Bill?

B.   No, I'm   not.

I called him   twice and he   didn't   answer.

I'm not going to   call him   again.

A.   Are you going to write to Sue?

B.   No, I'm   not.

I wrote to her   twice and she   didn't   answer.

I'm not going to   write her   again.

A.   Are you going to the   bank?

B.   No, I'm   not.

I went there   twice and it   wasn't   open.

I'm not going to   go there   again.

A.   Are you going to marry   Joan?

B.   No, I'm   not.

I asked her   twice and   she said   "No."

I'm not going to   ask her   again!

H. WHAT'S JUDY GOING TO GIVE HER FAMILY?

Judy is looking for presents for her family.
Here's what she's going to give them.

1. Her brother George loves sports. _____ *She's going to give him a football.* _____

2. Her Aunt Betty likes to read. _____

3. Her cousins Peter and Nancy really like to eat. _____

4. Her daughter likes to listen to music. _____

5. Her son is never on time. _____

6. Her grandmother loves clothes. _____

7. Her father and mother like to travel. _____

8. Her grandfather loves pets. _____

I. PRESENTS

1. Last year I _____*gave*_____ my husband
   a shirt.

   This year _____*I'm going to give him*_____
   a tie.

2. Last year Mary _____ her sister
   a doll.

   This year _____
   a bracelet.

3. Last year Jack _____ his father
   a briefcase.

   This year _____
   an umbrella.

4. Last year Mr. Smith _____ his
   children a bird.

   This year _____
   a cat.

5. Last year Mr. and Mrs. Jones _____
   their son a bicycle.

   This year _____
   clothes.

6. Last year Peter _____ his girlfriend
   a photograph.

   This year _____
   flowers.

7. Last year we _____ our mother and
   father candy.

   This year _____
   cookies.

8. Last year I ....

   This year ....

   ....

   ....

7

J. RHYTHM AND RHYME: *What Did You Give Them?*

Listen.   Then clap and practice.

A.   What did you give   Tommy for his   birthday?

B.   I gave him a   baseball   bat.

A.   Did he like it?   B. He said he   did.

But I think he really   wanted a   cat!

A.   What did you get   Sally for her   graduation?

B.   I got her a   black leather   coat.

A.   Did she like it?   B. She said she   did.

But I think she really   wanted a   boat!

A.   What did you buy your parents for their   anniversary?

B.   I bought them a   new   VCR.

A.   Did they like it?   B. They said they   did.

But I think they really   wanted a   car!

8

K. LISTEN Listen and write the correct activity under the appropriate date.

bowling	sailing	swimming
concert	football game	doctor
dentist	party	wedding

JULY

SUNDAY	MONDAY	TUESDAY	WEDNESDAY	THURSDAY	FRIDAY	SATURDAY
				1	2 bowling	3
4	5	6	7	8	9	10
11	12	13	14	15	16	17
18	19	20	21	22	23	24
25	26	27	28	29	30	31

L. LISTEN Listen and write the ordinal number you hear.

1. Peter Jones _____4th_____
2. the Smith family _____
3. The PRESTO Company _____
4. Mary Nelson _____
5. drug store _____
6. dentist's office _____
7. Barbara Harris and her son _____
8. Mr. and Mrs. Brown _____

9. Dr. Johnson _____
10. Mr. Jackson _____
11. Hilda Green _____
12. flower shop _____
13. Dr. Rinaldi _____
14. the Larson family _____
15. Mrs. Nathan _____
16. French restaurant _____

9

M. JOHNNY'S BIRTHDAYS

Fill in the missing words.

On Johnny's 7th birthday, his mother (take) _____took_____ him and his friends to the zoo.

1

After that, they all (go) _____ to a restaurant and (eat) _____ dessert. Johnny's friends

2   3

(love) _____ his birthday party, but Johnny was upset because his mother didn't

4

(buy) _____ him any candy at the zoo.

5

On Johnny's 10th birthday, he (have) _____ a picnic at the beach with his friends. They all

6

(play) _____ baseball and (go) _____ swimming. Johnny's friends

7   8

(love) _____ his birthday party, but Johnny was upset because he didn't (like)

9

_____ his presents. His friends (give) _____ him clothes and books, but Johnny

10   11

(want) _____ a football.

12

On Johnny's 13th birthday, he (have) _____ a party at home. His mother (cook)

13

_____ a big dinner, and his father (bake) _____ a cake. All his friends

14   15

(wish) _____ him "Happy Birthday." Johnny's friends (love) _____ his

16   17

birthday party, but Johnny was upset because the girls didn't (dance) _____. They

18

(sit) _____ and (talk) _____ and (watch) _____ TV.

19   20   21

On Johnny's 16th birthday, he didn't (have) _____ a party. He (go) _____

22   23

dancing with his girlfriend, and he (have) _____ a wonderful time. His friends didn't

24

(give) _____ him presents. His father didn't (bake) _____ him a cake. But

25   26

Johnny wasn't upset because his girlfriend (dance) _____ with him all night.

27

1. Why was Johnny upset on his 7th birthday? _____

_____

2. Why was he upset on his 10th birthday? _____

_____

3. Why was he upset on his 13th birthday? _____

_____

4. Was he upset on his 16th birthday? Why not? _____

_____

A. MISSING LABELS

Fill in the missing labels.

2

APPLES	BUTTER	EGGS	ONIONS
BANANAS	CHEESE	ICE CREAM	SODA
BREAD	COOKIES	MILK	SUGAR

1.

2.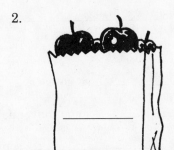
_____

3.

4.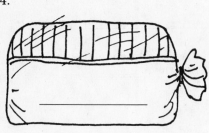
_____

5.
_____

6.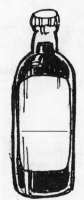
_____

7.
_____

8.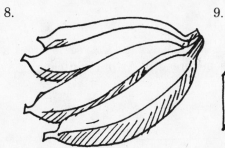
_____

9.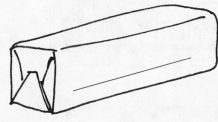
_____

10.
_____

11.
_____

12.
_____

11

B. LOOKING FOR FOOD

there's	there are

1. _____*There are*_____ some onions, _____*there's*_____ some

   pepper, and _____ some bananas in Jeff's kitchen.

2. _____ some beer, _____ some butter,

   _____ some mayonnaise, _____ some

   tomatoes, _____ some milk, and _____

   some apples in our refrigerator.

3. _____ some coffee, _____ some salt,

   and _____ some tea in Anita's kitchen.

4. _____ some ice cream and _____

   some yogurt in Linda's refrigerator.

5. _____ some sugar and _____

   some bread in Arthur's kitchen.

6. _____ some wine, _____ some eggs,

   _____ some lettuce, _____ some

   apples, _____ some melons, _____ some

   pears, and _____ some celery in Stanley's refrigerator.

7. _____ some soda, _____ some cheese,

   _____ some orange juice, _____ some

   jam, and _____ some jelly in Barbara's refrigerator.

12

C. I'M SORRY, BUT . . .

Look at the menu to see what Ed's Restaurant has and doesn't have today.

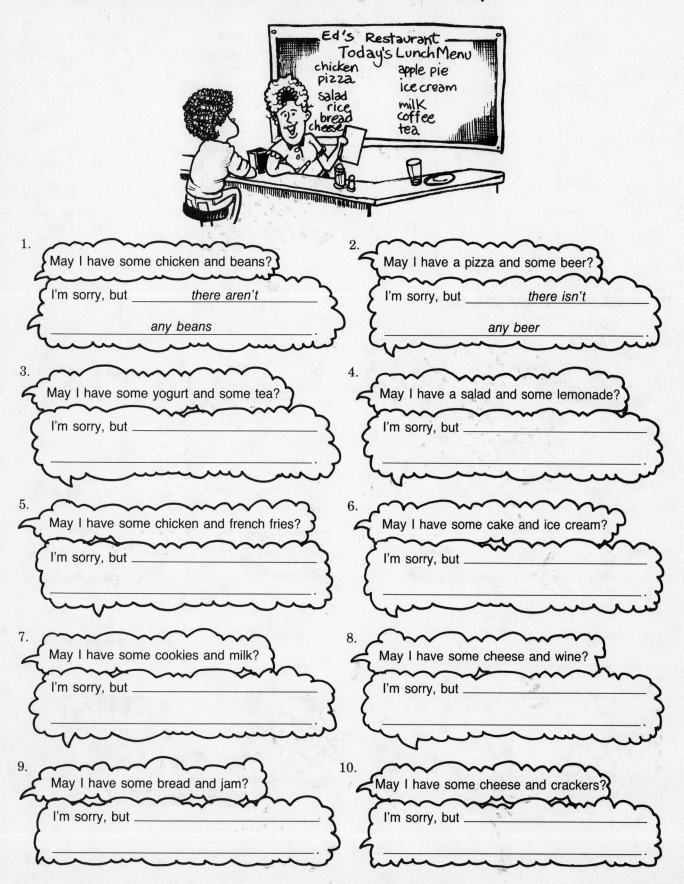

1.

May I have some chicken and beans?

I'm sorry, but _____ *there aren't* _____

_____ *any beans* _____ .

2.

May I have a pizza and some beer?

I'm sorry, but _____ *there isn't* _____

_____ *any beer* _____ .

3.

May I have some yogurt and some tea?

I'm sorry, but _____

_____ .

4.

May I have a salad and some lemonade?

I'm sorry, but _____

_____ .

5.

May I have some chicken and french fries?

I'm sorry, but _____

_____ .

6.

May I have some cake and ice cream?

I'm sorry, but _____

_____ .

7.

May I have some cookies and milk?

I'm sorry, but _____

_____ .

8.

May I have some cheese and wine?

I'm sorry, but _____

_____ .

9.

May I have some bread and jam?

I'm sorry, but _____

_____ .

10.

May I have some cheese and crackers?

I'm sorry, but _____

_____ .

13

Listen and put a circle around the correct word.

1. (isn't) / aren't   5. isn't / aren't   9. isn't / aren't   13. isn't / aren't

2. isn't / aren't   6. isn't / aren't   10. isn't / aren't   14. isn't / aren't

3. isn't / aren't   7. isn't / aren't   11. isn't / aren't   15. isn't / aren't

4. isn't / aren't   8. isn't / aren't   12. isn't / aren't   16. isn't / aren't

E. WHAT DO YOU WANT TO EAT?

1. There _____ *aren't any eggs* _____ .

How about some _____ *cereal* _____ ?

2. There _____ *isn't any chicken* _____ .

How about some _____ ?

3. There _____ .

How about some _____ ?

4. There _____ .

How about some _____ ?

5. There _____ .

How about some _____ ?

6. There _____ .

How about some _____ ?

7. There _____ .

How about some _____ ?

8. There _____ .

How about some _____ ?

F. HOME FROM VACATION

    The Jackson family got home this morning from their vacation.   They had a wonderful time, but they aren't feeling very well today.   Why not?

    What's the matter with Mr. Jackson?   Last night he went to an expensive restaurant with his family, and he ate too ⟨much⟩/many [1] dessert.   He ate so much/many [2] dessert that he's in bed today with a stomachache.

    Why do Alice and Jane Jackson feel terrible?   At the restaurant last night, Jane ate too much/many [3] garlic and too much/many [4] onions, and Alice ate too much/many [5] bread.   Alice ate so much/many [6] bread that she can't wear the new clothes she bought on vacation.   When she put on her new skirt this morning, it was too small.

    Mrs. Jackson and her son Robert didn't eat too much/many [7] food last night, but they don't feel very well either.   Mrs. Jackson is tired because she visited too much/many [8] churches and monuments yesterday, and she went to too much/many [9] stores.   Robert is tired because he wrote letters all morning and all afternoon on his last day of vacation.   He wrote so much/many [10] letters that he's never going to write a letter again.

What's the matter with John Jackson?   He feels terrible because he drank too [much / many] [11]

coffee last night.   He drank so [much / many] [12] coffee that he has a bad headache today.

Why does Linda Jackson look upset?   She's depressed because she bought too [much / many] [13]

expensive presents.   She bought so [much / many] [14] presents that she's going to have to work every day

after school this month.

1.   How [much / many] dessert did Mr. Jackson eat?   _____ *He ate so much dessert that he's* _____

_____ *in bed today with a stomachache.* _____

2.   How [much / many] bread did Alice eat?   _____

_____

3.   How [much / many] letters did Robert write?   _____

_____

4.   How [much / many] coffee did John drink?   _____

_____

5.   How [much / many] presents did Linda buy?   _____

_____

G. RHYTHM: *Just a Little, Just a Few*

Listen. Then clap and practice.

	•	•	•	•
A.	How much	salt should I	put in the	soup?
B.	Just	a little,	not too	much.
A.	How many	onions should I	put in the	salad?
B.	Just	a few,	not too	many.
A.	How much	pepper should I	put in the	stew?
B.	Just	a little,	not too	much.
A.	How many	eggs should I	put in the	omelette?
B.	Just	a few,	not too	many.
A.	How much	sugar should I	put in the	tea?
B.	Just	a little,	not too	much.

	•	•	•	•
All.	Salt in the	soup,		
	Pepper in the	stew,		
	Eggs in the	omelette,		
	Just	a few.		
	Just	a little,	not too	much.
	Not too	many,	just	a few.
	Just	a few,	not too	many,
	Not too	many,	just one or	two.

17

H. AT THE DINNER TABLE

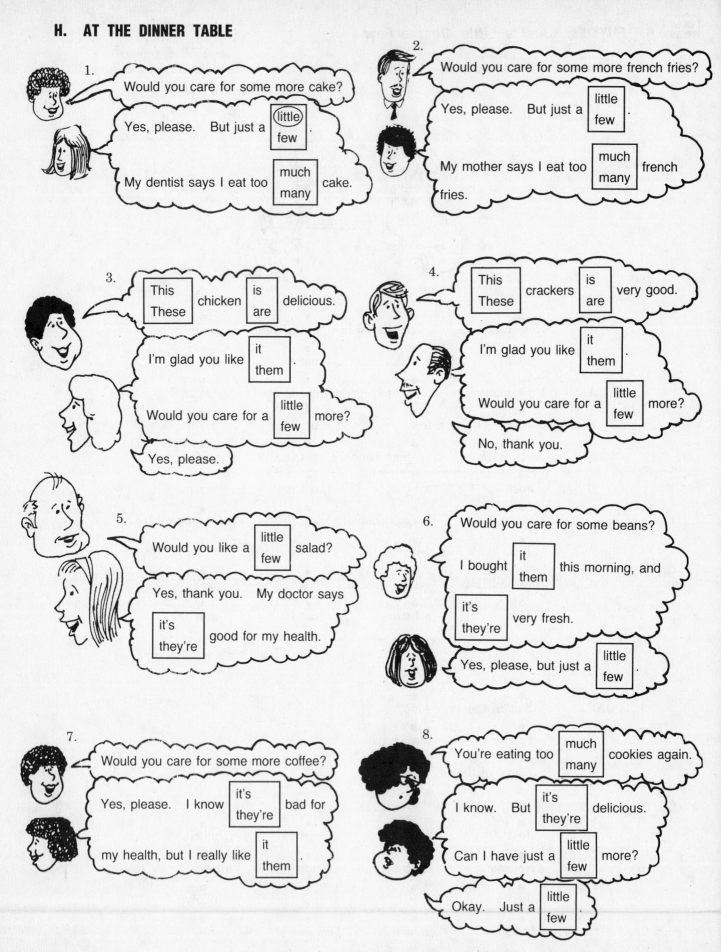

1.
Would you care for some more cake?

Yes, please. But just a [little/few].

My dentist says I eat too [much/many] cake.

2.
Would you care for some more french fries?

Yes, please. But just a [little/few].

My mother says I eat too [much/many] french fries.

3.
[This/These] chicken [is/are] delicious.

I'm glad you like [it/them].

Would you care for a [little/few] more?

Yes, please.

4.
[This/These] crackers [is/are] very good.

I'm glad you like [it/them].

Would you care for a [little/few] more?

No, thank you.

5.
Would you like a [little/few] salad?

Yes, thank you. My doctor says [it's/they're] good for my health.

6.
Would you care for some beans?

I bought [it/them] this morning, and [it's/they're] very fresh.

Yes, please, but just a [little/few].

7.
Would you care for some more coffee?

Yes, please. I know [it's/they're] bad for my health, but I really like [it/them].

8.
You're eating too [much/many] cookies again.

I know. But [it's/they're] delicious. Can I have just a [little/few] more?

Okay. Just a [little/few].

9.

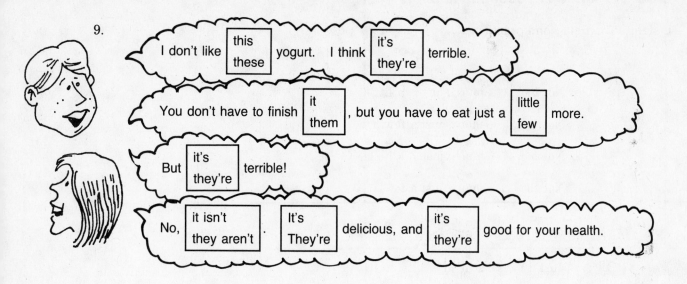

I don't like [this / these] yogurt. I think [it's / they're] terrible.

You don't have to finish [it / them], but you have to eat just a [little / few] more.

But [it's / they're] terrible!

No, [it isn't / they aren't]. [It's / They're] delicious, and [it's / they're] good for your health.

I. LISTEN

Listen and put a ✔ next to the correct picture.

1. ____✔____ _____

2. _____ _____

3. _____ _____

4. _____ _____

5. _____ _____

6. _____ _____

J. RHYTHM: *Second Helpings*

Listen. Then clap and practice.

All.	Not too	much, just	a little,
	Not too	many, just a	few.
	Not too	much, just	a little.
	Not too	many, just a	few.
A.	Would you	like more	chicken?
B.	Just	a little.	
A.	Would you	like more	carrots?
B.	Just	a few.	
A.	Would you	like more	gravy?
B.	Just	a little.	
A.	Would you	like more	mushrooms?
B.	Just	a few.	
A.	Would you	like more	salad?
B.	Just	a little.	
A.	Would you	like more tomatoes?	
B.	Just	a few.	
A.	Would you	like more	coffee?
B.	Just	a little.	
A.	Would you	like more	cookies?
B.	Just	a few.	
All.	Not too	much, just	a little,
	Not too	many, just a	few.
	Not too	much, just	a little,
	Not too	many, just a	few.

20

Listen.   Then clap and practice.

A.   My doctor   says I   can't have   sugar.

B.   There isn't any   sugar in   this.

A.   My doctor   says I   can't eat   eggs.

B.   There aren't any   eggs in   this.

A.   My doctor   says I   can't drink   milk.

B.   There isn't any   milk in   this.

A.   My doctor   says I   can't eat   wheat.

B.   There isn't any   wheat in   this.

A.   My doctor   says I   can't eat   bananas.

B.   There aren't any   bananas in   this.

A.   My doctor   says I   can't eat   meat.

B.   There isn't any   meat in   this.

A.   My doctor   says I   can't eat   strawberries.

B.   There aren't any   strawberries in   this.

A.   My doctor   says I   can't eat   fish.

B.   There isn't any   fish in   this.

A. SHOPPING LISTS

bag	bunch	head	loaf/loaves
bottle	can	jar	of
box	dozen	lb. (pound)	quart

1. Mary's friend is going to visit this afternoon.

> ### Mary's Shopping List
>
> a   _bottle_   _of_   soda
>
> a _____ _____ cookies
>
> a _____ _____ bread
>
> a _____ _____ butter
>
> a _____ _____ jam

2. Robert's friend is going to have lunch with him.

> ### Robert's Shopping List
>
> a _____ _____ milk
>
> a _____ _____ eggs
>
> ½ _____ _____ cheese
>
> a _____ _____ beans
>
> a _____ _____ lettuce
>
> a _____ _____ carrots

3. Jack is going to have a party tonight.

> ### Jack's Shopping List
>
> 2 _____ _____ wine
>
> 10 _____ _____ beer
>
> 1 _____ _____ ice cream
>
> 2 _____ _____ crackers
>
> a _____ _____ cheese
>
> a _____ _____ coffee
>
> 3 _____ _____ bananas

4. Eleanor is going to make a big lunch for her friends.

> ### Eleanor's Shopping List
>
> a _____ _____ flour
>
> a _____ _____ eggs
>
> a _____ _____ sugar
>
> a _____ _____ butter
>
> a _____ _____ apples
>
> 2 _____ _____ bread
>
> a _____ _____ mayonnaise
>
> 2 _____ _____ lettuce
>
> 2 _____ _____ carrots
>
> 3 _____ _____ wine

5. You're going to make a big dinner for your classmates. What are you going to buy?

```
┌─────────────────────────────────────┐
│           My Shopping List           │
│                                      │
│  .................................   │
│                                      │
│  .................................   │
│                                      │
│  .................................   │
│                                      │
│  .................................   │
│                                      │
│  .................................   │
│                                      │
│  .................................   │
│                                      │
│  .................................   │
└─────────────────────────────────────┘
```

B. LISTEN

Listen and write the prices you hear.

1. _____55¢_____

2. _____$1.80_____

3. _____

4. _____

5. _____

6. _____

7. _____

8. _____

9. _____

10. _____

11. _____

12. _____

Listen.   Then clap and practice.

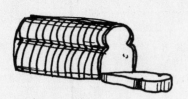

All.   We need   bread.

Whole wheat bread.

A.   How many   loaves do we need?

All.   Two.

All.   We need   beans.

Black   beans.

B.   How many   cans do we   need?

All.   Three.

All.   We need   rice.

Brown   rice.

C.   How many   pounds do we need?

All.   Four.

All.   We need   jam.

Strawberry   jam.

D.   How many   jars do we   need?

All.   Five.

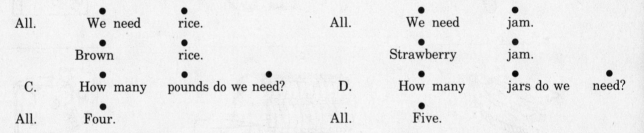

All.   We need   milk.

Fresh   milk.

E.   How many   quarts do we   need?

All.   Six.

All.   We need   cash.

We need   money.

F.   How much   money do we   need?

All.   A lot!

D. SHOPPING FOR FOOD

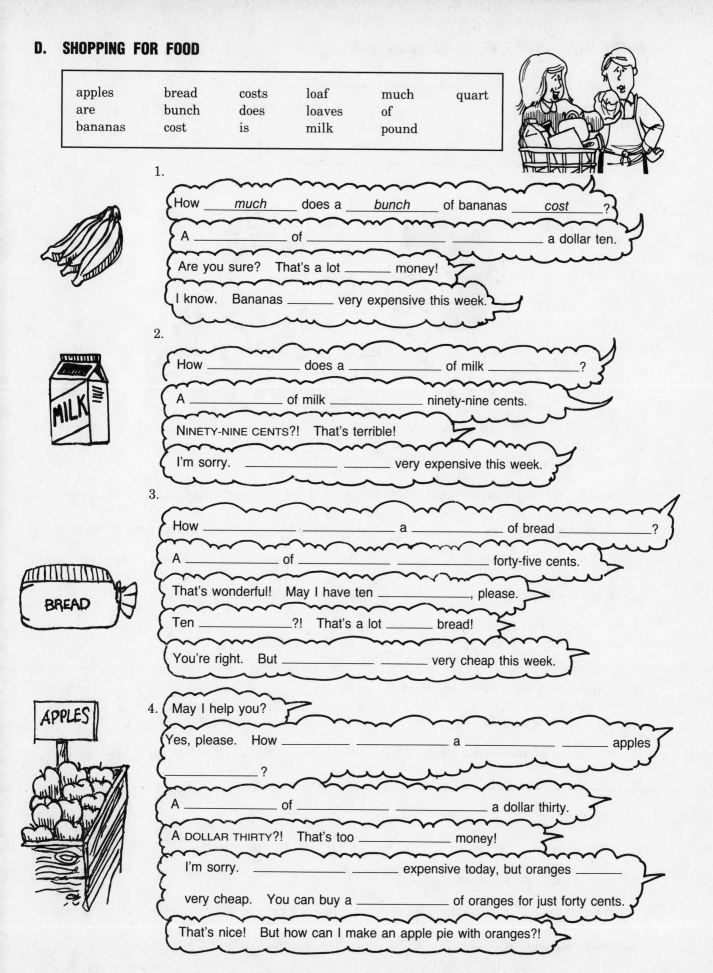

apples	bread	costs	loaf	much	quart
are	bunch	does	loaves	of	
bananas	cost	is	milk	pound	

1.

How _____*much*_____ does a _____*bunch*_____ of bananas _____*cost*_____?

A _____ of _____ a dollar ten.

Are you sure? That's a lot _____ money!

I know. Bananas _____ very expensive this week.

2.

How _____ does a _____ of milk _____?

A _____ of milk _____ ninety-nine cents.

NINETY-NINE CENTS?! That's terrible!

I'm sorry. _____ _____ very expensive this week.

3.

How _____ a _____ of bread _____?

A _____ of _____ forty-five cents.

That's wonderful! May I have ten _____, please.

Ten _____?! That's a lot _____ bread!

You're right. But _____ _____ very cheap this week.

4. May I help you?

Yes, please. How _____ _____ a _____ apples _____?

A _____ of _____ _____ a dollar thirty.

A DOLLAR THIRTY?! That's too _____ money!

I'm sorry. _____ expensive today, but oranges _____ very cheap. You can buy a _____ of oranges for just forty cents.

That's nice! But how can I make an apple pie with oranges?!

E. WHERE WOULD YOU LIKE TO GO FOR LUNCH?

are	cups	is	much	piece
bowl	dish	it	of	they
coffee	glass	many	order	

A. Where would you like to go for lunch?

B. Let's go to Henry's Restaurant. Their pancakes __are__ fantastic, and _____ aren't

1 2

expensive. I had an _____ _____ pancakes there last Saturday for a dollar fifty.

3 4

A. I don't want to go to Henry's Restaurant. Their pancakes _____ okay, but you can't get any

5

soup. I like to have a _____ _____ soup with my lunch.

6 7

B. How about Tom's Restaurant? Their soup _____ excellent, and _____ isn't expensive. A

8 9

_____ _____ soup costs fifty-nine cents.

10 11

A. I really don't like Tom's Restaurant. The soup _____ good, but their salad _____ terrible.

12 13

_____ has too _____ lettuce and too _____ onions.

14 15 16

B. How about Mario's Restaurant? Their desserts are wonderful. You can get a _____

17

_____ apple pie, a _____ _____ ice cream, or a _____ _____

18 19 20 21 22

strawberries.

A. I know, but their coffee _____ terrible. I like to have two or three _____ _____

23 24 25

_____ with my dessert.

26

B. Wait a minute! I know where we can go for lunch. Let's go to YOUR house!

A. That's a good idea.

F. LISTEN: *What Did They Have?*

Listen and write the missing words.

1. David usually has two ____*bowls*____ __*of*__ cereal for breakfast. This morning he got up

   late and had a _____ of _____.

2. Jane usually has a _____ _____ orange juice with her lunch. Yesterday, she had

   two _____ of _____.

3. Mr. Nelson usually has two _____ of _____ with his dinner.

   Yesterday he visited his Japanese neighbors and had a _____ _____ _____.

4. Peter usually has a _____ of _____ for lunch. Yesterday he was very

   hungry, and he had three _____ _____ chicken.

5. Lois usually has a _____ _____ yogurt for lunch. This afternoon she went to a

   restaurant and had two _____ _____ french fries.

6. Marie usually has a _____ of _____ for dessert. Yesterday she went to a

   party and had three _____ _____ ice cream.

7. Alice usually has a _____ _____ hot chocolate for breakfast. Yesterday morning she went

   to a restaurant and had an _____ of _____.

8. Nancy usually has a _____ of _____ for dessert. Yesterday she visited her

   grandmother and had two _____ of _____ and a _____ _____
   strawberries.

G. RHYTHM AND RHYME: *Grocery List*

Listen.   Then clap and practice.

We need a loaf of   bread
    And a jar of   jam,
      A box of   cookies
And a pound of   ham.
    A bottle of   ketchup,
    A pound of   cheese,
      A dozen   eggs,
And a can of   peas.
      A head of   lettuce,
Half a pound of rice,
    A bunch of   bananas,
And a bag of   ice.

H. RHYTHM AND RHYME: *What Would You Like to Have?*

Listen.   Then clap and practice.

A.   What would you like to   have?

B.   Hmm.   Let me see.

An order of   chicken,   a dish of   potatoes,

A large green   salad with a   lot of   tomatoes.

A bowl of   soup,   an order of   rice,

And a glass of   soda with a   lot of   ice.

A.   And what would you like for   dessert?

B.   Nothing,   thanks. I'm   not very   hungry!

I. BETTY'S DELICIOUS STEW

Put a circle around the correct words.

A. How do you make your delicious stew, Betty?

B. It's very easy. First I put a (little)/few [1] butter into a pan. Then I chop up a little/few [2] onions

and a little/few [3] garlic. After that, I cut up some chicken, and I add a little/few [4] salt and a

little/few [5] pepper. Then I cut up a little/few [6] tomatoes, and I slice a little/few [7] mushrooms.

Then I pour in a cup of wine and a little/few [8] chicken soup. I cook the stew for an hour.

Now fill in the correct words.

Betty's Recipe for Stew

1. _____*Put a little*_____ butter into a pan.

2. _____ onions and

   _____ garlic.

3. _____ some chicken.

4. _____ salt and _____ pepper.

5. _____ tomatoes.

6. _____ mushrooms.

7. _____ wine and

   _____ chicken soup.

8. _____ for an hour.

CHECK-UP TEST: *Chapters 1–3*

A. Put a circle around the correct word.

Ex. Cheese ⬚is／are⬚ expensive this week.

1. My dentist says I eat too ⬚much／many⬚ cookies.

2. She ate so ⬚much／many⬚ ice cream that she's

   going to have a stomachache tomorrow.

3. Would you care for a ⬚little／few⬚ beans?

   I bought ⬚it／them⬚ this morning and ⬚it's／they're⬚

   very fresh.

4. ⬚This／These⬚ rice ⬚is／are⬚ delicious.   May I have

   a ⬚little／few⬚ more?

5. How ⬚much／many⬚ does a pound of apples cost?

2. a _____ of
   _____

3. a _____ of
   _____

4. 2 _____ of
   _____

5. 2 _____ of
   _____

6. 2 _____ of
   _____

B. Fill in the blanks.

Ex. a _____*quart*_____ of
       _____*milk*_____

1. a _____ of
   _____

C. Complete the sentences.

Ex. Jane cooks spaghetti every week.

Last week _____*she cooked*_____ spaghetti.

Next week _____*she's going to cook*_____ spaghetti.

1. Johnny watches TV every evening.

   Yesterday evening he _____
   TV.

   Tomorrow evening _____
   TV.

2. I talk on the telephone every day.

Yesterday I _____
on the telephone.

Tomorrow _____
on the telephone.

3. Ed drinks coffee every morning.

Yesterday morning he _____
coffee.

Tomorrow morning _____
coffee.

4. We write to our uncle every week.

Last week we _____
to our uncle.

Next week _____
to our uncle.

5. Judy and Sara have a big birthday party every year.

Last year they _____
a big birthday party.

Next year _____
a big party.

6. We go skiing every winter.

Last winter we _____
skiing.

Next winter _____
skiing.

D. Complete the sentences.

Ex. Last year I gave my sister a necklace for her birthday.

This year _____*I'm going to give her*_____
earrings.

1. Last year we gave our neighbors flowers.

This year _____
candy.

2. Last year Mary gave her father a record.

This year _____
a briefcase.

3. Last year Billy gave his mother a book.

This year _____
perfume.

E. Listen and put a circle around the correct word.

"I'm sorry, but there _____ any."

Ex.
(isn't)
aren't

3.
isn't
aren't

1.
isn't
aren't

4.
isn't
aren't

2.
isn't
aren't

5.
isn't
aren't

A. SOON

4

1. Will the movie begin soon?

Yes, _____*it will*_____ . _____*It'll*_____ _____*begin*_____ in a few minutes.

2. Will Uncle Albert be here soon?

Yes, _____ . _____ in a little while.

3. Will Mr. and Mrs. Smith return soon?

Yes, _____ . _____ in an hour.

4. _____ your mother _____ soon?

Yes, _____ . _____ get up in a little while.

5. _____ dinner _____ soon?

Yes, _____ . _____ be ready in a few minutes.

6. Will you _____ your homework soon?

Yes, _____ . _____ finish it in an hour.

7. _____ Mary and Bob _____ _____ soon?

Yes, _____ . _____ get married next month.

8. _____ you _____ soon?

Yes, _____ . _____ get out of the hospital in a few days.

B. WHAT DO YOU THINK?

YES!   NO!

1. What will Mary study next year?

Maybe _____ _she'll_ _____

_____ _study_ _____ French.

I'm sure _____ _sh_ ____

won't study _____ ᴧnish.

2. When will Billy call his uncle?

Maybe _____ him tomorrow.

I'm sure ____ _____

_____ ᴧim tonight.

3. What will your children have for dessert?

Maybe _____ some ice cream.

I'm sure _____

_____ any pie.

4. Where will you and Sally go this evening?

Maybe _____

_____ to a concert.

I'm sure _____

_____ to a movie again.

5. Where will George live next year?

Maybe _____ in New York.

I'm sure _____

_____ at home.

6. Do you think it'll be cold tomorrow?

Maybe _____ cold.

I'm sure _____

_____ hot.

7. When will you finish your homework?

Maybe _____ it tomorrow.

I'm sure _____

_____ it tonight.

8. Who will Jane go out with on Saturday?

Maybe _____

_____ with Robert.

I'm sure _____

_____ with Fred.

9. What do you think you'll get for your birthday?

Maybe _____ some books.

I'm sure _____

_____ clothes.

10. What will Mr. and Mrs. Peterson plant in their garden?

Maybe _____

_____ tomatoes.

I'm sure _____

_____ flowers.

11. When will the train arrive?

Maybe _____ in half an hour.

I'm sure _____

_____ on time.

12. When will Mr. and Mrs. Smith move to Miami?

Maybe _____ there in ten years.

I'm sure _____

_____ there soon.

13. When will we finish our English book?

Maybe _____ it in a few months.

I'm sure _____

_____ it very soon.

33

C. WRITE AND SAY IT

Write and say the sentences.

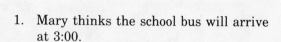

1. Mary thinks the school bus will arrive at 3:00.

   Her husband thinks _____ *it'll arrive* at 4:00.

2. Mary thinks Uncle Harry will call tonight.

   Her husband thinks _____ tomorrow.

3. Mary thinks her neighbors will move to New York.

   Her husband thinks _____ to Boston.

4. Mary thinks their daughter will be an actress.

   Her husband thinks _____ a violinist.

5. Mary thinks the children will be home soon.

   Her husband thinks _____ late again.

6. Mary thinks the car will be ready today.

   Her husband thinks _____ next week.

D. LISTEN

Listen and put a circle around the words you hear.

1. won't / (want to)

2. won't / want to

3. won't / want to

4. won't / want to

5. won't / want to

6. won't / want to

7. won't / want to

8. won't / want to

9. won't / want to

10. won't / want to

11. won't / want to

12. won't / want to

13. won't / want to

14. won't / want to

15. won't / want to

E. RHYTHM AND INTONATION: *You'll See*

Listen. Then clap and practice.

A. I'll remember.

B. Are you sure?

A. Don't worry. I'll remember. You'll see.

A. He'll do it.

B. Are you sure?

A. Don't worry. He'll do it. You'll see.

A. She'll call you.

B. Are you sure?

A. Don't worry. She'll call you. You'll see.

A. It'll be ready.

B. Are you sure?

A. Don't worry. It'll be ready. You'll see.

A. We'll be there.

B. Are you sure?

A. Don't worry. We'll be there. You'll see.

A. They'll get here.

B. Are you sure?

A. Don't worry. They'll get here. You'll see.

F. WE DON'T KNOW

1. When are you going to do your homework? [tonight] [tomorrow]

   _____I might do my homework tonight_____ , or _____I might do my homework tomorrow_____ .

2. What's Jack going to do this afternoon? [go sailing] [go swimming]

   _____ , or _____

3. What time is Betty going to get up this morning? [10:00] [11:00]

   _____ , or _____

4. Where are you and Anna going to go on your vacation? [Paris] [London]

   _____ , or _____

5. Who is Nancy going to visit this afternoon? [grandmother] [aunt]

   _____ , or _____

6. What are you going to give your sister for her birthday? [necklace] [bracelet]

   _____ , or _____

7. What are Bob and Judy going to do tonight? [listen to music] [play cards]

   _____ , or _____

8. What kind of food are you and David going to eat tonight? [Chinese] [Greek]

   _____ , or _____

9. What's Michael going to be when he grows up? [doctor] [dentist]

   _____ , or _____

10. When are Mr. and Mrs. Wilson going to return from their vacation? [on Sunday] [next week]

   _____ , or _____

G. LOUD AND CLEAR

Fill in the words.   Then read the sentences aloud.

warm	wearing	Williams	winter

walk	wet	Winston	won't

1. Mrs. _____*Williams*_____ is _____*wearing*_____

   a _____*warm*_____ _____*winter*_____ coat.

2. Mr. _____ _____

   _____ there because the

   floor is _____ .

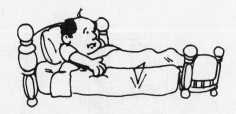

wasn't	Wednesday	well	William

wash	William	Wednesday
wife	windows	

3. _____ _____

   at work on _____

   because he didn't feel _____ .

4. _____ and his _____

   _____ their _____

   every _____ .

wait	Walter	war	wife	will

swimming	wanted	warm
wasn't	we	weather

5. _____ will fight in the

   _____ . Walter's _____

   _____ have to _____

   at home.

6. _____ _____ to go

   _____ , but the

   _____ _____

   _____ .

H. PESSIMISTS

break her leg	get carsick	have too much homework
catch a cold	get fat	look terrible
fall asleep	get home very late	miss their train
get a backache	get seasick	rain
get sunburn	go to jail	step on her feet
	have noisy neighbors	

1. Jack won't go sailing because

   he's afraid he might

   get seasick .

2. Tom won't play basketball because

   _____ .

3. Helen won't take a walk in the park because

   _____

   _____ .

4. We won't live in an apartment building

   because _____

   _____ .

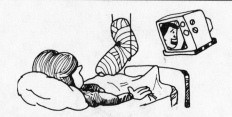

5. Barbara won't go skiing because

   _____

   _____ .

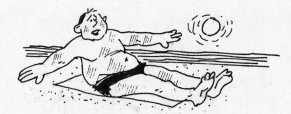

6. Albert won't go to the beach because

   _____

   _____ .

7. Steven won't wash his clothes today because

   _____

   _____ .

8. Sally won't take a ride with me because

   _____

   _____ .

9. Jennifer won't take English next year in school because _____

_____ .

10. Fred won't eat any dessert because

_____

_____ .

11. George and his brother won't have lunch with us this afternoon because _____

_____ .

12. Jim won't go dancing with Patty because

_____

_____ .

13. David won't go to the movies tonight because _____

_____ .

14. Frank won't get a haircut because

_____

_____ .

15. Ronald won't go to Peggy's party this Saturday night because _____

_____ .

16. I won't steal cars any more because

_____

_____ .

Listen.   Then clap and practice.

A.   When is he going to leave?

B.   He might leave at   noon.

C.   He might leave on   Monday.

D.   He might leave in   June.

A.   Where is he going to go?

B.   He might go to   Spain.

C.   He might go to   Texas.

D.   He might go to   Maine.

A.   How is he going to   get there?

B.   He might go by   train.

C.   He might take the   bus.

D.   He might take a   plane.

A.   Who is he going to   go with?

B.   He might go with   Ed.

C.   He might go with   Peter.

D.   He might go with   Fred.

A.   What's he going to   do there?

B.   He might see the   zoo.

C.   He might take some   pictures.

D.   He might write to   you.

40

A. OLD AND NEW

1. My old house was large.   My new house is _____larger_____ .

2. Linda's old car was fast.   Her new car is _____ .

3. My old sofa was soft.   My new sofa is _____ .

4. Our old apartment building was clean.   Our new apartment building is _____ .

5. My old briefcase was light.   My new briefcase is _____ .

6. Mrs. Black's old hat was fancy.   Her new hat is _____ .

7. My old neighbors were friendly.   My new neighbors are _____ .

8. Jane's old school was big.   Her new school is _____ .

9. Shirley's old bicycle was safe.   Her new bicycle is _____ .

10. Jack's old watch was cheap.   His new watch is _____ .

11. My old earrings were pretty.   My new earrings are _____ .

12. Walter's old job was easy.   His new job is _____ .

13. Billy's old mittens were warm.   His new mittens are _____ .

14. Jeff's old records were noisy.   His new records are _____ .

15. Sara's old coat was heavy.   Her new coat is _____ .

16. Helen's old neighborhood was quiet.   Her new neighborhood is _____ .

17. Our old doctor was always busy.   Our new doctor is _____ .

18. Dan's old shirt was white.   His new shirt is _____ .

19. Rita's old cat was always hungry.   Her new cat is _____ .

20. My old English book was short.   My new English book is _____ .

21. Fred's old dog was fat.   His new dog is _____ .

B. THEY'RE DIFFERENT

1. My uncle is energetic, but my cousin is _____*more energetic*_____ .

2. Mrs. Smith's apple pie is delicious, but my mother's apple pie is _____ .

3. My brother is intelligent, but his girlfriend is _____ .

4. Our furniture is comfortable, but our neighbor's furniture is _____ .

5. Mary's husband is handsome, but her son is _____ .

6. My children are smart, but my sister's children are _____ .

7. Uncle Albert is rich, but Uncle Edward is _____ .

8. Herman is hungry, but Harry is _____ .

9. Sally's apartment is attractive, but George's apartment is _____ .

10. My suitcase is light, but my brother's suitcase is _____ .

11. Our stove is dirty, but our neighbor's stove is _____ .

12. Paul's teeth are white, but his dentist's teeth are _____ .

13. My pet bird is beautiful, but Betty's bird is _____ .

14. Tommy's hair is short, but his barber's hair is _____ .

15. Aunt Mary is old, but Uncle Bob is _____ .

16. Yesterday was hot, but today is _____ .

17. Henry is thin, but his girlfriend is _____ .

18. Bill's clothes are expensive, but his roommate's clothes are _____ .

19. My children are healthy, but my doctor's children are _____ .

20. My feet are large, but my father's feet are _____ .

C. WHAT SHOULD THEY DO?

buy new clothes	call the police	get a wig	go to the doctor
call a mechanic	drink tea	go on vacation	move to a
call the plumber	get a job	go to the dentist	new apartment

1. The sink in Walter's bathroom is broken.

    He should call the plumber.

2. Mary has a toothache.

    _____

3. Mr. and Mrs. Smith don't like their new apartment building.

    _____

4. Mr. Jones worked every day this year, and he's very tired.

    _____

5. Billy is much bigger this year.   His old clothes are too small.

    _____

6. Doris has a headache and a stomachache.

    _____

7. Jack's car is broken and he can't fix it.

    _____

8. My doctor says coffee isn't good for my health.

    _____

9. A thief stole Mr. and Mrs. Johnson's car.

    _____

10. Martha wants to buy a motorcycle, but she doesn't have much money.

    _____

11. I think my hair looks terrible.

    _____

D. PUExamZLE

D. PUZZLE

Grid with 1 across "newer" filled in. Numbered cells: 1, 2, 3, 4, 5, 6, 7, 8, 9, 10, 11, 12, 13, 14.

Across

1. John's car is older than Helen's car. Helen's car is _____ than John's car.
2. Our kitchen is smaller than our bedroom. Our bedroom is _____ than our kitchen.
4. Barbara is always sick. Frieda is never sick. Frieda is _____ than Barbara.
5. Dogs really like to be with people. They're _____ than cats.
8. Yesterday was 95°F. Today is 90°F. Yesterday was _____ than today.
9. We cleaned our apartment today. Yesterday our apartment was _____ .
11. Mario's Restaurant is fancy, but Pierre's Restaurant is _____ .
12. My sister is younger than I am. I'm _____ than my sister.
13. Peter has a lot of money. He's _____ than his friends.
14. Peter's friends don't have much money. They're _____ than Peter.

Down

1. Ted is quieter than Walter. Walter is _____ than Ted.
2. George works every day. Mark rarely works. Mark is _____ than George.
3. Chapter 5 is more difficult than Chapter 4. Chapter 4 is _____ than Chapter 5.
5. Jack eats too much cake and candy. That's why he's _____ than his brothers.
6. Anita put PRESTO Floor Wax on her floor yesterday, and now it's _____ than before.
7. William always travels by train because he thinks trains are _____ than planes.
10. Last year Tommy was short, but this year he's _____ .

44

E. RHYTHM AND RHYME: *Honey Is Sweeter than Sugar*

Listen. Then clap and practice.

Honey is	sweeter than	sugar.	
Coffee is	stronger than	tea.	
Hours are	longer than	minutes.	
Thirty is	larger than three.		

Peaches are	softer than	apples.	
Pepper is	hotter than	rice.	
Oranges are	bigger than	lemons.	
Nothing is	colder than	ice.	

F. RHYTHM AND RHYME: *I Can't Decide*

Listen. Then clap and practice.

I can't decide   who to go   out with.
Bob is more   interesting than Bill.
Tom is more   handsome than   Tony.
And Frank's more   exciting than   Phil.

I can't decide   who to go   out with.
Alice is more   talented than   Anne.
Sue's more   attractive than   Sally.
And Jane's more   exciting than   Jan.

G. RHYTHM AND RHYME: *Should I . . . ?*

Listen. Then clap and practice.

A.   Should he   call or   should he   write?

B.   He should   call   tomorrow   night.

A.   Should I   keep it or   give it   back?

B.   You should   wear it or   give it to   Jack.

A.   Should I   stay or   should I   go?

B.   Don't ask   me.   I don't know.

H. YOU DECIDE

fast	safe

1. Should I take a plane or a train?

I think _____*you should take a plane*_____

because _____*planes are faster than trains*_____

(or)

I think _____*you should take a train*_____

because _____*trains are safer than planes*_____ .

beautiful	quiet

2. Should Mary live in San Juan or San Miguel?

I think _____

because _____ .

fancy	cheap

3. Should Paul go to Stanley's Restaurant or
Joe's Restaurant?

I think _____

because _____ .

convenient	clean

4. Should Bill live on Main Street or Garden Street?

I think _____

because _____ .

Dan

Michael

friendly	intelligent

5. Should I go out on a date with Dan or Michael?

I think _____

because _____

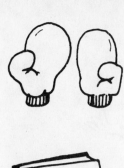

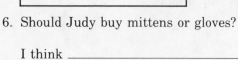

warm	attractive

6. Should Judy buy mittens or gloves?

I think _____

because _____ .

easy	interesting

7. Should David do his French homework or his mathematics homework?

I think _____

because _____ .

 I. LISTEN

Listen and put a circle around the correct answer.

 yes / no

1. George   Jennifer

  yes / no

2. Albert   John

  yes / no

3. Ted's dog   Fred and Sally's dog

  yes / no

4. Robert   Nancy

  yes / no

5. English test   French test

  yes / no

6. Alice   Margaret

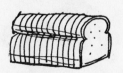 yes / no

7. $1.15 $1.05

 yes / no

8. Bob   Bill

▭ J. RHYTHM: *What Should They Do?*

Listen. Then clap and practice.

A.   What should I   do?
      Should I buy this   car?
B.   I think you can   find something cheaper.

A.   What should we   do?
      Should we rent this   apartment?
B.   I think you can   find something   larger.

A.   What should he   wear?
      Should he wear this   jacket?
B.   I think he should   wear something   warmer.

A.   What should they   do?
      Should they take the   bus?
B.   I think they should   take something   faster.

A.   What should she   do?
      Should she marry her   boss?
B.   I think she can   find someone   nicer.

48

K. WHAT'S THE WORD

mine	ours
his	yours
hers	theirs

1. Is that John's bicycle?

   No. It isn't ____*his*____.

2. Is that Mr. and Mrs. Smith's car

   No. It isn't _____.

3. Are those your mother's earrings?

   No. They aren't _____.

4. Is that my recipe for vegetable soup?

   No. It isn't _____.

5. Are these Johnny's shoes?

   No. They aren't _____.

6. Are these Maria's boots?

   No. They aren't _____.

7. Is that your dog?

   No. It isn't _____.

L. DIFFERENT, BUT OKAY

1. John (rich) _____*isn't as rich as*_____ Tom, but he's much (happy) _____*happier*_____.

2. Our apartment (clean) _____ Rita's apartment, but it's

   much (comfortable) _____.

3. Linda's children (intelligent) _____ Maria's children,

   but they're much (healthy) _____.

4. My room (large) _____ my sister's room, but it's

   much (pretty) _____.

5. Our neighborhood (safe) _____ Steve's neighborhood, but

   it's much (interesting) _____.

6. George's dog (smart) _____ Fred's dog, but he's

   much (friendly) _____.

7. Walter (handsome) _____ Tim, but he's

   much (nice) _____.

(continued) 49

8. My computer (powerful) _____ Jennifer's computer, but it's

   much (cheap) _____ .

9. Betty's car (new) _____ Carol's car, but it's

   much (shiny) _____ .

10. Mrs. Green (young) _____ Sally, but she's

    much (energetic) _____ .

11. This rug (expensive) _____ Bob's rug, but it's

    much (soft) _____ .

12. Ed's car (big) _____ Jeff's car, but it's

    much (good) _____ .

M. YOU'RE RIGHT

1. Peggy isn't as talented as Ginger.

   You're right.   Ginger is ___*more*___

   ___*talented than*___ Peggy.

2. English isn't as difficult as Arabic.

   You're right.   Arabic is _____

   _____ English.

3. Dr. Smith isn't as busy as Dr. Brown.

   You're right.   Dr. Brown is _____

   _____ Dr. Smith.

4. Toronto isn't _____ Mexico City.

   You're right.   Mexico City is noisier than Toronto.

5. Bill's apartment isn't _____

   _____ Roger's apartment.

   You're right.   Roger's apartment is bigger than Bill's apartment.

6. Betty isn't as beautiful as her mother.

   You're right.   Betty's mother is

   _____ Betty.

7. My suitcase isn't _____

   _____ yours.

   You're right.   Mine is lighter than yours.

8. Miguel isn't _____ Carlos.

   You're right.   Carlos is nicer than Miguel.

N. RHYTHM AND RHYME: *Ticket Mix-Up*

Listen. Then clap and practice.

Where's my ticket?
Who has mine?
I don't want to
stand in line.

Who has hers?
Who has his?
I wonder where
my ticket is!

He has his.
I have mine.
She has hers.
Everything's fine!

O. RHYTHM AND RHYME: *His Job Is Easy*

Listen. Then clap and practice.

His job is easy,
Hers is, too.
Mine's a more difficult job to do.
His job's as simple
as A B C.
Mine requires a P H D.

51

P. WHO SHOULD WE HIRE?

Fill in the missing words.

A. Do you think we should hire Miss Jackson?   Everybody says she's capable and honest.

B. I know.   Miss Jackson is very honest, but how about Mrs. Wilson?   I think she's (interesting)

   _____*more interesting*_____ than Miss Jackson, and she's much (smart) _____.

1
2

A. I agree.   Mrs. Wilson is very intelligent, but in my opinion, she isn't as (smart) _____

3

   as Mr. Brown.   Maybe we should give Mr. Brown the job.

B. No.   I really don't think so.   Mr. Brown is (lively) _____ than Miss

4

   Jackson, but he isn't as (capable) _____ as Mrs. Wilson.   You know, I think

5

   Mr. Smith is the right person for the job.   He's (talented) _____

6

   than Miss Jackson, he's (polite) _____ than Mr. Brown,

7

   and he's (friendly) _____ than Mrs. Wilson.

8

A. Do you think he's as (intelligent) _____ as Mr. Brown?

9

B. I think so.   And he isn't as (talkative) _____.

10

A. You're right.   He's (good) _____ for the job than Miss Jackson, Mrs. Wilson,

11

   or Mr. Brown.   Let's hire him!

52

Q. DO YOU AGREE?

I agree.
I disagree.
I agree/disagree with
  (you, him, her, John . . .).

I think so.
I don't think so.
In my opinion, . . .

Tom: I think Chinese food is more delicious than Italian food.

George: I disagree with you.   I think Italian food is much more delicious than Chinese food.

1. What's Tom's opinion? _____

2. Does George agree? _____

3. Do YOU agree with Tom or with George?   Why? ....

....

Anita: I think dogs are smarter than cats.

Edward: I don't think so.   In my opinion, cats are much smarter than dogs.

4. Does Edward agree with Anita? _____

5. What's Edward's opinion? _____

6. What's YOUR opinion? ....

Robert: In my opinion, English is more useful than Latin.

Anna: I disagree.   I think Latin is more useful than English.

Miguel: I agree with Robert.

7. What does Robert think? _____

8. Does Anna agree with him? _____

9. What does Miguel think? _____

10. What do YOU think?   Why? ....

....

A. WHAT DO YOU THINK?

6

1. Do you think I'm pretty?

   You certainly are. You're _____the prettiest_____ girl I know.

2. Do you think Johnny is lazy?

   Yes. In my opinion, he's _____ student in the class.

3. Is Mary's new apartment large?

   Yes, it is. It's _____ _____ apartment in the building.

4. I think Aunt Martha is very kind.

   I agree. She's _____ _____ person in our family.

5. Is Uncle Walter rich?

   He sure is. He's _____ _____ person I know.

6. Is Jack's new motorcycle safe?

   I think so. It's _____ _____ motorcycle you can buy.

7. I think Billy is very funny.

   I think so, too. He's _____ little boy I know.

8. My sister is very sloppy.

   She certainly is. She's _____ person I know.

9. Is Albert really shy?

   Yes, he is. _____ person I know.

10. Is your new baby big?

    He sure is. He's _____ baby in the hospital!

B. WHAT'S THE WORD?

boring	energetic	honest	lazy	polite	stubborn
bright	generous	interesting	patient	stingy	talented

1. Steve always says "thank you."   He's very _____ *polite* _____.

   In fact, he's _____ *the most polite* _____ person I know.

2. Helen is a wonderful violinist.   She's very _____.

   In fact, she's _____ person I know.

3. Peter always buys expensive gifts for his friends.   He's very _____.

   In fact, he's _____ person I know.

4. Harry swims every day before work.   He's very _____.

   In fact, he's _____ person I know.

5. Tom never does his homework.   He's very _____.

   In fact, he's _____ boy I know.

6. My boss never wants to give me more money.   He's very _____.

   In fact, he's _____ person I know.

7. Betty never gets angry.   She's very _____.

   In fact, she's _____ person I know.

8. My cousin Alice always talks about the weather.   She's very _____.

   In fact, she's _____ person I know.

9. Sally knows the answers to all the questions.   She's very _____.

   In fact, she's _____ person I know.

10. Uncle Robert always says what he thinks.   He's very _____.

    In fact, he's _____ person I know.

11. I'm never bored when I'm with Mary.   She's very _____.

    In fact, she's _____ person I know.

12. Henry is always sure he's right.   He's very _____.

    In fact, he's _____ person I know.

C. AROUND THE WORLD

Gloria Green is the wealthiest woman in Centerville. She loves to go shopping. Last year she traveled around the world and bought presents for all her friends and family.

1. (attractive) She bought a purse in Rome because she thinks Italian purses are

   _____*the most attractive*_____ purses in the world.

2. (soft) She bought leather gloves in Madrid because she thinks Spanish gloves are

   _____ gloves in the world.

3. (beautiful) She bought a gold bracelet in Athens because she thinks Greek bracelets are

   _____ bracelets in the world.

4. (warm) She bought a fur hat in Moscow because she thinks Russian hats are

   _____ hats in the world.

5. (modern) She bought some furniture in Stockholm because she thinks Swedish furniture

   is _____ furniture in the world.

6. (elegant) She bought an evening gown in Paris because she thinks French evening gowns

   are _____ evening gowns in the world.

7. (pretty) She bought a Chinese rug in Hong Kong because she thinks Chinese rugs are

   _____ rugs in the world.

8. (good) She bought a suit in London because she thinks English suits are

   _____ suits in the world.

9. (safe) She bought a car in Tokyo because she thinks Japanese cars are

   _____ cars in the world.

10. (reliable) She bought a watch in Geneva because she thinks Swiss watches are

    _____ watches in the world.

11. She also bought .... in .... because she thinks ....

    ....

D. RHYTHM AND RHYME: *What Do You Think About . . . ?*

Listen.   Then clap and practice.

A.   What do you   think about   Kirk?

B.   He's the friendliest   person at   work!

A.   What do you   think about   Flo?

B.   She's the most patient   person I   know!

A.   What do you   think about   Pete?

B.   He's the nicest   boy on the   street!

A.   What do you   think about   Kate?

B.   She's the most talented   teacher in the   state!

A.   What do you   think about   Bob?

B.   He's the laziest   guy on the   job!

A.   What do you   think about   Frank?

B.   He's the most polite   teller at the   bank!

A.   What do you   think about   Nellie?

B.   She's the fastest   waitress at the   deli!

A.   What do you   think about this   kitty?

B.   It's the ugliest   cat in the   city!

57

E. WONDERFUL PRESTO PRODUCTS

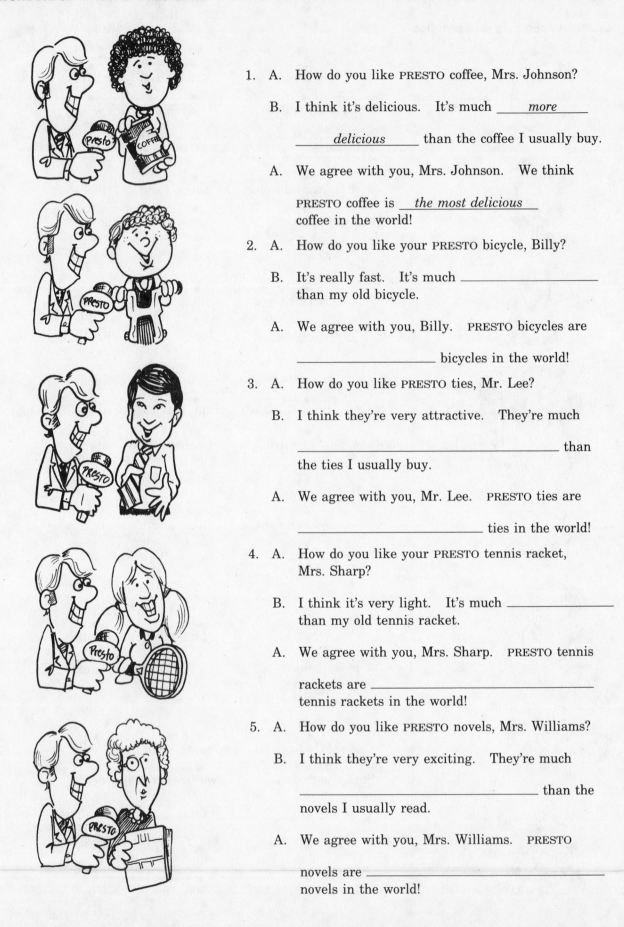

1. A. How do you like PRESTO coffee, Mrs. Johnson?

   B. I think it's delicious. It's much ___more___ ___delicious___ than the coffee I usually buy.

   A. We agree with you, Mrs. Johnson. We think PRESTO coffee is _the most delicious_ coffee in the world!

2. A. How do you like your PRESTO bicycle, Billy?

   B. It's really fast. It's much _____ than my old bicycle.

   A. We agree with you, Billy. PRESTO bicycles are _____ bicycles in the world!

3. A. How do you like PRESTO ties, Mr. Lee?

   B. I think they're very attractive. They're much _____ than the ties I usually buy.

   A. We agree with you, Mr. Lee. PRESTO ties are _____ ties in the world!

4. A. How do you like your PRESTO tennis racket, Mrs. Sharp?

   B. I think it's very light. It's much _____ than my old tennis racket.

   A. We agree with you, Mrs. Sharp. PRESTO tennis rackets are _____ tennis rackets in the world!

5. A. How do you like PRESTO novels, Mrs. Williams?

   B. I think they're very exciting. They're much _____ than the novels I usually read.

   A. We agree with you, Mrs. Williams. PRESTO novels are _____ novels in the world!

6. A. How do you like your PRESTO fan, Mr. Nathan?

   B. I think it's very quiet. It's much _____ than my old fan.

   A. We agree with you, Mr. Nathan. PRESTO fans are

   _____ fans in the world!

7. A. How do you like PRESTO shampoo, Mrs. Schultz?

   B. I think it's wonderful. Now my hair is soft and shiny.

   It's much _____ and _____ than before.

   A. We agree with you, Mrs. Schultz. Women who wash

   with PRESTO shampoo have _____

   _____ and _____
   hair in the world!

8. A. How do you like PRESTO soap, Mrs. Rinaldi?

   B. I think it's terrific. My clothes are so clean and

   fresh. They're much _____

   and _____ than before.

   A. We agree with you, Mrs. Rinaldi. People who
   wash with PRESTO soap have

   _____ and _____
   clothes in the world!

9. A. How do you like this PRESTO cake, Mary?

   B. I think it's good. It's much _____
   than the cakes I usually eat.

   A. We agree with you, Mary. PRESTO cakes are

   _____ cakes in the world!

10. A. How do you like your PRESTO wig, Mrs. Harris?

    B. I think it's beautiful. It's much _____

    _____ than my old wig.

    A. We agree with you, Mrs. Harris. PRESTO wigs are

    _____ wigs in the world!

F. LOUD AND CLEAR

Fill in the words. Then read the sentences aloud.

favorite	ironing	Robert	shirt

brother	German	our	write

1. _____*Robert*_____ is _____*ironing*_____

his ___*favorite*___ ____*shirt*____ .

2. _____ little _____

can read and _____ _____ .

better	recipe	rice	right

are	arrive	morning	mother
		Rome	

3. You're _____ ! Barbara's

_____ for _____ is

_____ than mine.

4. My _____ and father _____

going to _____ from _____

next Thursday _____ .

attractive	birthday	her
racket	received	thirtieth

broken	Friday	Mr.	radiator
Roberts	their	very	were

5. Sara _____ an

_____ tennis

_____ for _____

_____ .

6. _____ and Mrs. _____

_____ _____ cold last

_____ because _____

_____ was _____ .

60

G. RHYTHM: *Who's the Best Student in Our English Class?*

Listen. Then clap and practice.

All. Who's the best student
in our English class?

A. HE'S the best,
Better than the rest!

B. I'm not the best!
I'm not the best!
SHE'S the best,
Better than the rest!

C. I'm not the best!
I'm not the best!
YOU'RE the best,
Better than the rest!

D. I'm not the best!
I'm not the best!
YOU'RE . . . .

CHECK-UP TEST: *Chapters 4–6*

A. Complete the sentences.

Ex. Will you be back soon?

Yes, _____*I will*_____. __I'll__
be back in fifteen minutes.

Ex. Will George be home soon?

No, _____*he won't*_____. He's
busy tonight.

1. Will the movie begin soon?

Yes, _____. _____
begin in a few minutes.

2. Will Aunt Helen get out of the hospital
soon?

No, _____. She's very
sick.

3. Will you be ready soon?

Yes, _____. _____
be ready in a little while.

4. Will the boss be in the office tomorrow?

No, _____. He's on
vacation.

5. Will your friends be here soon?

Yes, _____. _____
be here in half an hour.

B. Complete the sentences with *might* or *should*.

```
might        should
```

1. I don't think I'll go swimming with you.

I'm afraid I _____
drown.

2. What do you think? _____
I buy a bicycle or a motorcycle?

3. I _____ get married next

month, or I _____ get
married next year.   I really can't decide.

4. John's doctor thinks he _____
drink milk because it's good for him.

C. Fill in the blanks.

Ex. A. Are these Betty's glasses?

B. No. They aren't _____*hers*_____.

1. A. Is that Fred's English book?

B. No. It isn't _____.

2. A. Is this your car?

B. No. It isn't _____.

3. A. Is that Mr. and Mrs. Wong's house?

B. No. It isn't _____.

4. A. Are these my gloves?

B. No. They aren't _____.

D. Fill in the blanks.

Ex. Dan is _____*nicer than*_____ Bill.

    nice

1. Michael is _____ John.

           tall

2. Carol is _____ Judy.

          capable

3. My dog is _____

           friendly
your dog.

4. Joe's bicycle is _____

                 fast
Tim's bicycle.

5. Patty's cake is _____

                 delicious

_____ my cake.

E. Complete the sentences.

Ex. John (rich) _____*isn't as*_____

_____*rich as*_____ Carl, but he's

much (happy) _____*happier*_____ .

1. Henry's neighborhood (interesting)

_____

Jack's neighborhood, but it's much

(safe) _____ .

2. Elizabeth (nice) _____

_____ Katherine, but

she's much (talented) _____ .

3. Doris (young) _____

_____ Jane, but she's

much (healthy) _____ .

4. My apartment (elegant) _____

_____ your

apartment, but it's much (big)

_____ .

5. Tom's car (new) _____
Lee's car, but it's much (good)

_____ .

F. Fill in the blanks.

Ex. Harry is _____*the kindest*_____ person I
know.   kind

1. Mary is _____ person I
know.   nice

2. Uncle Herbert is _____

_____ person in

our family.   intelligent

3. Bill has _____ apartment
in the neighborhood.   large

4. Mrs. Blake is _____
teacher in our school.   interesting

5. Jack is _____ person
I know.   honest

G. Listen and put a circle around the correct answer.

Ex. Alice   [Yes / No]   Margaret

1. Bob   [Yes / No]   Bill

2. [Yes / No]

3. Herman   [Yes / No]   David

4. 100°F/38°C   [Yes / No]   32°F/0°C
   Madrid   Stockholm

5. Jack   [Yes / No]   Carl

63

A. HOW DO I GET THERE?

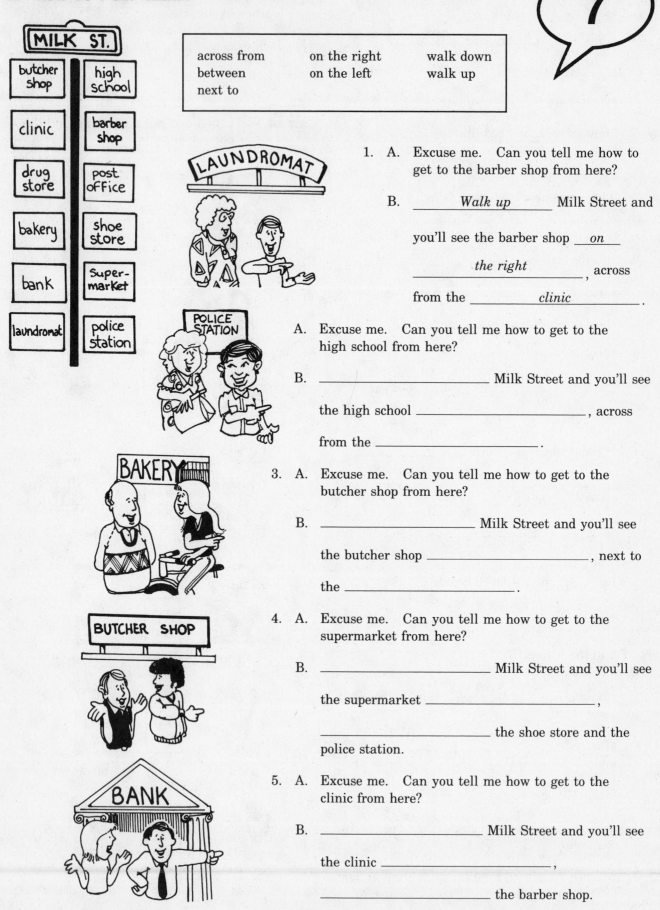

MILK ST.

butcher shop	high school
clinic	barber shop
drug store	post office
bakery	shoe store
bank	super-market
laundromat	police station

across from	on the right	walk down
between	on the left	walk up
next to		

1. A. Excuse me.   Can you tell me how to get to the barber shop from here?

    B. _____*Walk up*_____ Milk Street and you'll see the barber shop _____*on*_____

    _____*the right*_____, across from the _____*clinic*_____.

2. A. Excuse me.   Can you tell me how to get to the high school from here?

    B. _____ Milk Street and you'll see the high school _____, across

    from the _____.

3. A. Excuse me.   Can you tell me how to get to the butcher shop from here?

    B. _____ Milk Street and you'll see the butcher shop _____, next to

    the _____.

4. A. Excuse me.   Can you tell me how to get to the supermarket from here?

    B. _____ Milk Street and you'll see the supermarket _____,

    _____ the shoe store and the police station.

5. A. Excuse me.   Can you tell me how to get to the clinic from here?

    B. _____ Milk Street and you'll see the clinic _____,

    _____ the barber shop.

64

B. WHICH WAY?

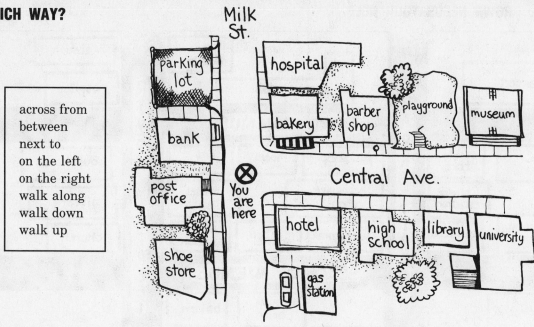

across from
between
next to
on the left
on the right
walk along
walk down
walk up

1. A. Excuse me. Could you please tell me how to get to the library from here?

   B. _____*Walk along*_____ Central Avenue and you'll see the library _____*on the right*_____,

   across from the _____*playground*_____.

2. A. Excuse me. Could you tell me how to get to the museum from here?

   B. _____ Central Avenue and you'll see the museum

   _____, across from the _____.

3. A. Excuse me. Can you please tell me how to get to the parking lot from here?

   B. _____ Milk Street and you'll see the parking lot

   _____, _____ the hospital.

4. A. Excuse me. Can you tell me how to get to the shoe store from here?

   B. _____ Milk Street and you'll see the shoe store

   _____, _____ the post office.

5. A. Excuse me. How do I get to the university from here?

   B. _____ Central Avenue and you'll see the university

   _____, next to the _____.

6. A. Excuse me. Can you tell me how to get to the playground from here?

   B. _____ Central Avenue and you'll see the playground

   _____, _____ the

   _____ and the _____.

C. MRS. BROWN NEEDS YOUR HELP

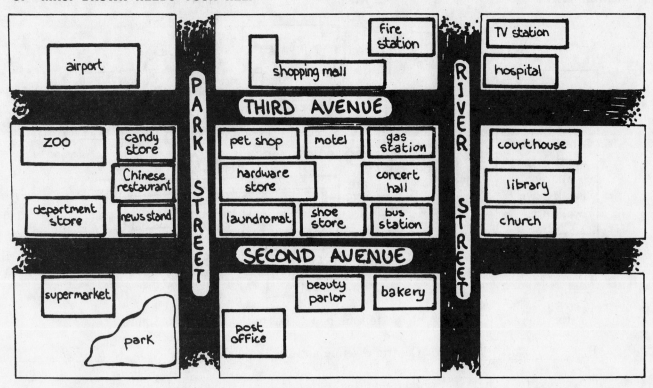

Mrs. Brown is very busy today. She has to go to several stores, but she doesn't know the city very well. She needs YOUR help.

1. She's at the post office, and she's going to the bakery because she wants to buy fresh bread. Tell her how to get there.

_____*Walk up*_____ Park Street to Second Avenue and _____*turn right*_____.

_____*Walk along*_____ Second Avenue and you'll see the bakery

_____*on the right*_____, _____*across from*_____ the bus station.

2. She's at the bakery, and she wants to go to the hardware store because she has to fix her sink.

_____ Second Avenue to Park Street and _____

_____. _____ Park Street and you'll see the hardware

store _____, _____ the pet shop and the laundromat.

3. She's at the hardware store, and she's going to the shopping mall because she needs a raincoat.

_____ Park Street to Third Avenue and _____.

_____ Third Avenue and you'll see the shopping mall

_____, _____ the motel.

66

4. She's at the shopping mall, and she's very hungry. She wants to go to the Chinese restaurant for lunch.

_____ Third Avenue to Park Street and _____ .

_____ Park Street and you'll see the Chinese restaurant

_____ , _____ the candy store.

5. Mrs. Brown is at the Chinese restaurant, and she wants to go to the library to get a book.

_____ Park Street to Second Avenue and _____ .

_____ Second Avenue to River Street and _____ .

_____ River Street and you'll see the library _____

_____ , _____ the _____ and the _____ .

6. She's at the library, and she wants to go to the shoe store. She's looking for a more comfortable pair of shoes.

....

....

....

7. She's at the shoe store, and now she has to visit a friend in the hospital.

....

....

....

8. Mrs. Brown is very tired, and she wants to sit in the park and rest before she goes home.

....

....

....

Thank you for your help.

Listen.   Then clap and practice.

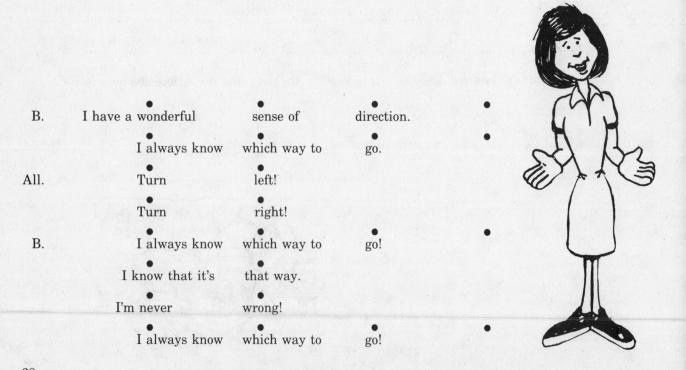

A.   I have a terrible   sense of   direction.
     I never know   which way to   go!

All.   This way or   that way?
       This way or   that way?

A.   I never know   which way to   go!
     I think that it's   that way, but   maybe I'm   wrong.
     I never know   which way to   go!

B.   I have a wonderful   sense of   direction.
     I always know   which way to   go.

All.   Turn   left!
       Turn   right!

B.   I always know   which way to   go!
     I know that it's   that way.
     I'm never   wrong!
     I always know   which way to   go!

E. IN A HURRY

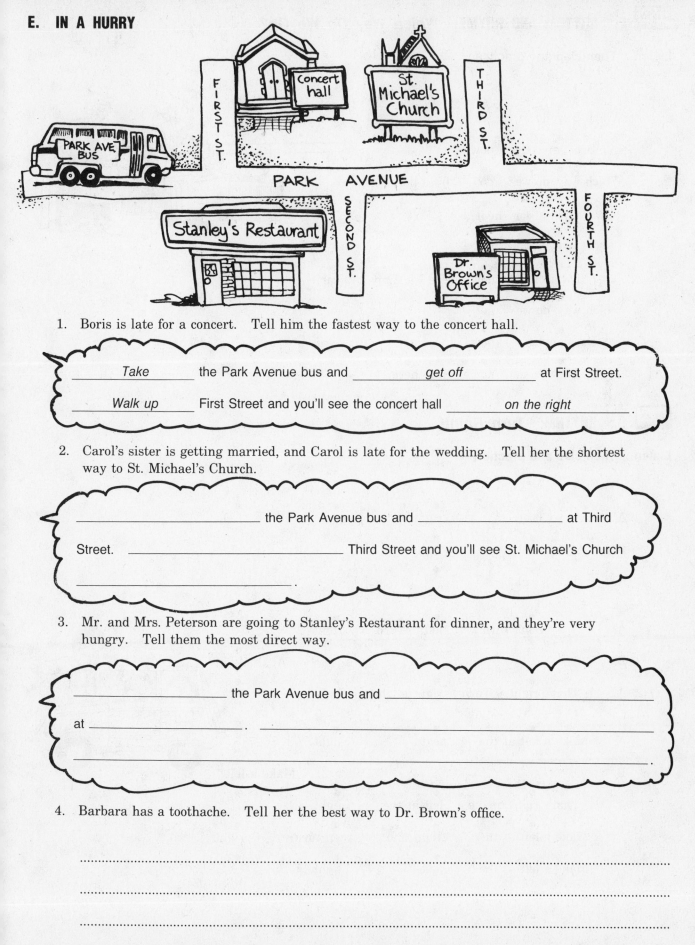

1. Boris is late for a concert. Tell him the fastest way to the concert hall.

   _____*Take*_____ the Park Avenue bus and _____*get off*_____ at First Street.

   _____*Walk up*_____ First Street and you'll see the concert hall _____*on the right*_____.

2. Carol's sister is getting married, and Carol is late for the wedding. Tell her the shortest way to St. Michael's Church.

   _____ the Park Avenue bus and _____ at Third Street. _____ Third Street and you'll see St. Michael's Church _____ .

3. Mr. and Mrs. Peterson are going to Stanley's Restaurant for dinner, and they're very hungry. Tell them the most direct way.

   _____ the Park Avenue bus and _____ at _____ . _____ .

4. Barbara has a toothache. Tell her the best way to Dr. Brown's office.

   ....

   ....

   ....

F. RHYTHM AND RHYME: *Which Way Do We Go?*

Listen.   Then clap and practice.

Which way do we go?

Does anybody know?

Which way do we go from here?

Is it very near?

Is it very far?

I wish I knew where I left my car!

Which way do we go?

Does anybody know

how to get home from here?

G. RHYTHM: *Turn Right!*

Listen.   Then clap and practice.

A.   Turn right at the next light.

B.   At the next light?

A.   That's right.

A.   Don't turn left! Turn right!

B.   At the light?

A.   That's right. Turn right at the light.

A.   Make a left at the next light.

B.   Make a left?

A.   That's right, make a left at the light.

Make a left at the light and then turn right.

Make a left at the next light.

70

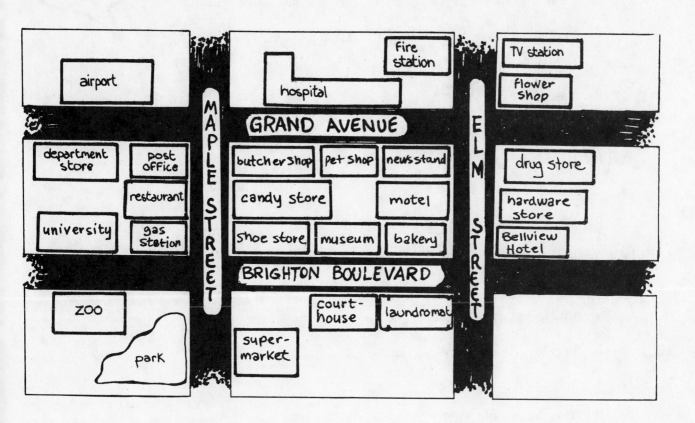

Listen and fill in the correct places.

1. He went to the _____ .

2. She went to the _____ .

3. They went to the _____ .

4. He went to the _____ .

5. She went to the _____ .

6. They went to the _____ .

7. They went to the _____ .

A. WHAT DO YOU THINK?

8

1. A. I think Gloria is a terrible tennis player. What do you think?

    B. I agree. She plays tennis _____*terribly*_____ .

2. A. Is Arthur a graceful dancer?

    B. Yes. He dances very _____ .

3. A. I think Frank is a careless driver.

    B. He certainly is. He drives very _____ .

4. A. Is Rita a slow worker?

    B. Yes. She works very _____ .

5. A. Is Natasha an accurate translator?

    B. She certainly is. She translates everything very _____ .

6. A. I think Charlie is a very sloppy eater.

    B. I agree. He eats very _____ .

7. A. Is Susan a fast swimmer?

    B. Yes, she is. She swims very _____ .

8. A. Is your mother a good baker?

    B. She certainly is. She bakes very _____ .

9. A. I think Shirley is a _____ skater. What do you think?

    B. I agree. She skates beautifully.

10. A. I think Mr. Green is a _____ worker.

    B. I think so, too. He works very patiently.

11. A. Is George a _____ football player?

    B. Yes. He plays football very well.

12. A. Is Roger a hard worker?

    B. Yes. He works very _____ .

B. ANSWER

Put a circle around the correct word.

1. George is a [**terrible** / terribly] painter.   He paints very [sloppy / (**sloppily**)].

2. I don't like to play cards with Harry.   He plays very [dishonest / dishonestly].

3. Richard is a [slow / slowly] chess player, but he plays very [good / well].

4. Frieda is very [graceful / gracefully].   She dances [beautiful / beautifully].

5. According to Mario, you can live [cheap / cheaply] in Rome.

6. Michael plays tennis [terrible / terribly], but he's a [good / well] baseball player.

7. Anna plays the violin very [bad / badly], but her family listens [patient / patiently].

8. I usually drive [careful / carefully], but I was very [careless / carelessly] yesterday.

C. LISTEN

Listen and put a circle around the correct answer.

1. [(**neat**) / neatly]

2. [sloppy / sloppily]

3. [accurate / accurately]

4. [beautiful / beautifully]

5. [graceful / gracefully]

6. [bad / badly]

7. [sloppy / sloppily]

8. [elegant / elegantly]

9. [safe / safely]

10. [slow / slowly]

11. [careful / carefully]

12. [easy / easily]

D. RHYTHM: *How Am I Doing?*

Listen. Then clap and practice.

A. How am I   doing?

Am I driving   all right?

B. You're driving very   carefully.

You're driving very   well.

A. How am I   doing?

Am I singing   all right?

B. You're singing very beautifully.

You're singing very   well.

A. How am I   doing?

Am I dancing   all right?

B. You're dancing very   gracefully.

You're dancing very   well.

A. How am I   doing?

Am I working   all right?

B. You're working very   hard.

You're working very   well.

E. THE BOSS IS ANGRY

Fill in the correct words.

early	_____*earlier*_____	neat(ly) { _____	_____ }
careful	_____*more carefully*_____		
late	_____	politely	_____
loud(ly) { _____	_____ }	slowly { _____	_____ }

1. A. Mr. Smith, I think you dress too sloppily.

   B. You're right, Mr. Sharp. I'll try to dress { *more neatly* / _____*neater*_____ }.

2. A. I also think you speak too softly.

   B. You're right, Mr. Sharp. I'll try to speak _____.

3. A. And, Mr. Smith, I think you get to the office too late.

   B. You're right, Mr. Sharp. I'll try to get to the office _____.

4. A. And I'm upset, Mr. Smith, because you type too carelessly.

   B. You're right, Mr. Sharp. I'll try to type _____.

5. A. Also, Mr. Smith, everybody says you speak too quickly.

   B. You're right, Mr. Sharp. I'll try to speak _____.

6. A. And before you leave, Mr. Smith, I want to tell you that everybody is upset because you go home too early.

   B. You're right, Mr. Sharp. I'll try to go home _____.

   A. That's all, Mr. Smith. You can go now.

   B. Thank you, Mr. Sharp.

7.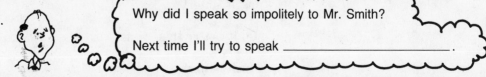

   Why did I speak so impolitely to Mr. Smith?

   Next time I'll try to speak _____.

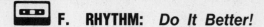

F. RHYTHM: *Do It Better!*

Listen.   Then clap and practice.

A.   Try it   again,
         faster this   time!

B.   Faster than this?

A.   Much faster!

A.   Type it   again,
         neater this   time!

B.   Neater than this?

A.   Much neater!

A.   Say it   again,
         slower this   time!

B.   Slower than   this?

A.   Much slower!

A.   Sing it   again,
         softer this   time.

B.   Softer than   this?

A.   Much softer!

All.   Try it faster!

          Type it neater!

          Say it slower!

          Sing it softer!

          Do it better this time!

          Much better!

G. WHAT'S THE WORD?

1. If ⟨I move⟩ / I'll move to Boston, I live / ⟨I'll live⟩ on Main Street.

2. If you call / you'll call your mother, she'll be very happy.

3. If the mechanic fixes our car on time, we drive / we'll drive to Centerville.

4. If it rains / it'll rain today, we won't go to the park.

5. If I'm not in a hurry tonight, I write / I'll write to her.

6. If she isn't / won't be sick, she'll go to school.

7. If they're / they'll be tired tomorrow, they don't go / won't go to work.

8. If John doesn't buy a new car, he buys / he'll buy a motorcycle.

H. IF

1. If we __go__ to London, ____we'll____ visit our cousin.

2. If they _____ their homework tonight, their teacher _____ happy.

3. If the weather _____ good, George _____ swimming this weekend.

4. If he _____ swimming this weekend, _____ a wonderful time.

5. If you don't eat your dinner tonight, _____ hungry.

6. If _____ tired, they'll go to sleep early tonight.

7. If it _____, she'll wear her new raincoat.

8. If you _____ too many cookies after dinner tonight, _____ get a stomachache.

9. If I _____ too much coffee, _____ get a headache.

10. If we _____ a boy, _____ him Peter.

77

I. SCRAMBLED SENTENCES

Unscramble the sentences.

1. if   she   she'll   misses   bus   the   walk

   _____*If she misses the bus*_____ , _____*she'll walk*_____ .

2. if   he   he'll   concert   goes   his   suit,   the   to   wear

   _____ , _____ .

3. if   she   she'll   cook   isn't   dinner   tired

   _____ , _____ .

4. if   I'm   I'll   busy   not   you   visit

   _____ , _____ .

5. if   you   you'll   be   don't   school   finish   sorry

   _____ , _____ .

6. if   he   he'll   a   get   good   hard   job   works

   _____ , _____ .

J. YOU DECIDE

Complete the sentences with any vocabulary you wish.

1. If the weather is bad tomorrow, ...

2. If we hitchhike to work, ...

3. If I don't sleep well tonight, ...

4. If you don't fix the broken window, ...

5. If he doesn't cut his hair, ...

6. If ...., they'll go to a restaurant tonight.

7. If ...., his mother will be happy.

8. If ...., his mother will be sad.

9. If ...., her boss will fire her.

10. If ...., their friends will be angry.

78

K. RHYTHM AND RHYME: *If You Leave at Six*

Listen.   Then clap and practice.

If you leave at   six,
You'll be there at   eight.
If you don't leave now,
You'll be very   late.

If you start work now,
You'll be through at   seven.
If you wait 'till   noon,
You'll be busy 'till   eleven.

If you catch the train,
You'll be home by   ten.
If you get there   late,
You'll miss dinner   again.

L. RHYTHM AND RHYME: *Party Guests*

Listen.   Then clap and practice.

A.   I'll ask   Bob if   you ask   Bill.

B.   I'll bring   Tom if   you bring   Jill.

A.   I'll call   Susan if   you call   Tim.

B.   I'll call   Janet if   you ask   Jim.

A.   If I ask   Jim, I'll   have to ask   Sue.

B.   If you ask   Sue, you'll   have to ask   Lou.

A.   If I ask   Lou, he'll   want to bring   Bella.

B.   If you don't ask   Bella, you   can't ask   Stella.

A.   If I ask   Jane, will I   have to ask   Phil?

B.   You'll have to ask   Phil, and you'll have to ask   Bill.

M. YOU DECIDE: *What Might Happen?*

1. Margaret shouldn't sing so loudly.

   If she sings too loudly, she might ....

2. Paul shouldn't eat so much.

   If he eats too much, he might ....

3. Your friends shouldn't do their homework so quickly.

   If they do their homework too quickly, they might ....

4. Richard shouldn't worry so much.

   If he worries too much, he might ....

5. You shouldn't ski so carelessly.

   If ....

6. Your husband shouldn't speak so impolitely to his boss.

   If ....

7. Your children shouldn't go to bed so late.

   If ....

8. Bill shouldn't play his radio so loud.

   If ....

9. Betty shouldn't play cards so dishonestly.

   If ....

10. You shouldn't talk so much.

    If ....

N. PLEASE DON'T

1. Please don't bake an apple pie for dessert!

Why not?

If you bake an apple pie for dessert, I'll eat too much.

If ____*I eat*____ too much, ____*I'll*____ get fat.

And if _____ fat, _____ have to buy new clothes.

So please don't bake an apple pie for dessert!

2. Please don't play your stereo so loud!

Why not?

If you play your stereo too loud, the neighbors will be upset.

If _____ upset, _____ tell the landlord.

And if _____ the landlord, _____ get angry.

So please don't play your stereo so loud!

3. Please don't buy Tommy a science fiction book!

Why not?

If you buy him a science fiction book, he'll read all night.

If _____ all night, _____ be tired in the morning.

If _____ tired in the morning, he won't get up on time.

If _____ get up on time, _____ be late for school.

And if _____ late for school, _____ miss his English test.

So please don't buy Tommy a science fiction book!

81

CHECK-UP TEST: *Chapters 7–8*

A. Complete the sentences.

Ex. He's a careless driver.

He drives very _____*carelessly*_____.

1. She's a graceful dancer.

She dances very _____.

2. He's a terrible soccer player.

He plays soccer _____.

3. They're sloppy eaters.

They eat very _____.

4. We're hard workers.

We work very _____.

B. Put a circle around the correct answer.

1. She's not a $\boxed{\begin{array}{l}\text{good}\\ \text{well}\end{array}}$ tennis player.   She plays

tennis $\boxed{\begin{array}{l}\text{bad}\\ \text{badly}\end{array}}$.

2. Mary types $\boxed{\begin{array}{l}\text{quick}\\ \text{quickly}\end{array}}$, but she isn't

$\boxed{\begin{array}{l}\text{accurate}\\ \text{accurately}\end{array}}$.

3. I don't dress $\boxed{\begin{array}{l}\text{beautiful}\\ \text{beautifully}\end{array}}$, but I

dress $\boxed{\begin{array}{l}\text{neat}\\ \text{neatly}\end{array}}$.

4. John usually drives $\boxed{\begin{array}{l}\text{safe}\\ \text{safely}\end{array}}$, but

yesterday he was $\boxed{\begin{array}{l}\text{careless}\\ \text{carelessly}\end{array}}$.

C. Complete the sentences.

Ex. Edward dresses too sloppily.

He should try to dress ____ $\left\{\begin{array}{l}\textit{more neatly}\\ \textit{neater}\end{array}\right\}$ ____.

1. Albert leaves work too early.

He should try to leave work _____.

2. Linda speaks too impolitely.

She should try to speak _____.

3. Alice works too slowly.

She should try to work _____.

4. Peter talks too softly.

He should try to talk _____.

D. Complete the sentences.

Ex. If they ____*have*____ a girl, ____*they'll*____ name her Jane.

1. If the weather _____ good, we'll go sailing on Saturday.

2. If you _____ TV too much,

_____ get a headache.

3. If _____ hungry tonight, I'll eat a big dinner.

4. If Tommy _____ his homework

tonight, his teacher _____ happy.

E. Put a circle around the correct answer.

1. If $\boxed{\begin{array}{l}\text{we go}\\ \text{we'll go}\end{array}}$ to the supermarket this

afternoon, $\boxed{\begin{array}{l}\text{we buy}\\ \text{we'll buy}\end{array}}$ some bread.

82

2. If it [won't / doesn't] rain tomorrow, [she'll go / she goes] swimming.

3. If I eat too much tonight, I [get / might get] a stomachache.

4. If my parents [will feel / feel] better tonight, they [visit / might visit] our neighbors.

F. Listen and fill in the correct places.

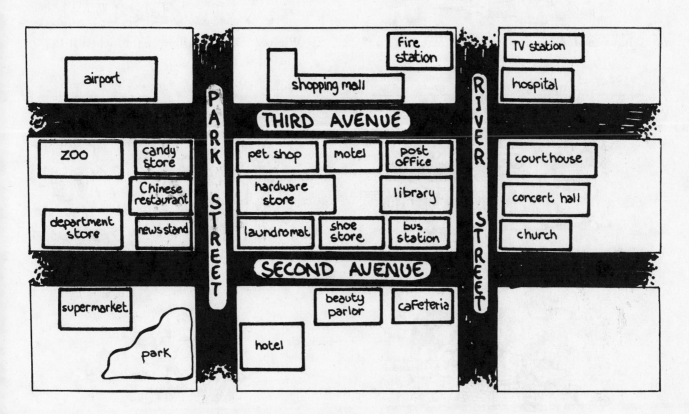

1. She went to the _____.

2. He went to the _____.

3. They went to the _____.

4. She went to the _____.

5. They went to the _____.

A. BAD WEATHER

have a picnic	play baseball	swim	wait for the bus
plant flowers	ride her bicycle	take a walk	wash her car

Yesterday morning it was sunny and beautiful, but at 1:00 in the afternoon it started to rain.

1. What was Janet doing when it started to rain?

_____ *She was washing her car.* _____

2. What was Mr. Williams doing when it started to rain?

_____

3. What were you and Mary doing?

_____

4. What was Michael doing?

_____

5. What were your friends doing?

_____

6. What was Nancy doing?

_____

7. What were Mr. and Mrs. Blake doing?

_____

8. What was your brother doing?

_____

9. What were YOU doing?

....

B. RHYTHM: *We Were All Having a Wonderful Time*

Listen.   Then clap and practice.

We were singing and dancing and standing   around,
　　　Singing and dancing and standing   around.
We were singing and dancing and
　　　Singing and dancing and
　　　Singing and dancing and standing   around.

Susan was   singing,
Danny was   dancing,
Stella and   Stanley were standing   around.

Lucy was   laughing,
Tommy was   talking,
Stuart and   Steven were standing   around.

We were all   having a   wonderful   time.
We were all   having a   wonderful   time.
　　　Singing and dancing and laughing and talking,
We were all   having a   wonderful   time.

85

C. WHAT WERE THEY DOING?

1. They (wait) _____*were waiting*_____ for the bus when it started to snow.

2. She (wash) _____ her hair when her boyfriend called.

3. They (play) _____ cards when their parents got home.

4. I (take) _____ a bath when the plumber arrived.

5. We (leave) _____ the movie theater when we saw our English teacher.

6. She (look for) _____ her purse when the lights went out.

7. My children (make) _____ breakfast when we got up.

8. He (talk) _____ to his friend when the teacher asked him a question.

D. WHAT'S THE WORD?

1. When I saw John, he was getting
| on |
| off |
| (into) |
a taxi.

2. George was walking
| out of |
| off |
| of |
the library when he saw his brother.

3. Anna got
| from |
| off |
| up |
the bus and walked home.

4. We walked
| into |
| out of |
| in |
the nearest restaurant because we were hungry.

5. Get
| at |
| up |
| on |
the subway at First Avenue.

6. Helen was riding her bicycle
| through |
| along |
| in |
Main Street.

7. I'm going to get
| out of |
| off |
| into |
the car because I'm feeling carsick.

E. TOO EARLY

Jim was embarrassed  when he arrived at his girlfriend Mary's house for dinner last night.   He got there MUCH too early, and Mary and her family weren't ready.

1. What was Mary doing when Jim arrived?

    She was cleaning the living room.

2. What was Mary's mother doing?

3. What was Mary's father doing?

4. What were her little brother and sister doing?

5. What was her older sister Betty doing?

6. What was her brother Paul doing?

Listen. Then clap and practice.

A.   I called you   all day   yesterday,

     But you never   answered your phone.

B.   That's strange! I was there from   morning 'till night.

     I was home all day   all alone.

A.   What were you doing when I called at nine?

B.   I was probably hanging my clothes on the line.

A.   What were you doing when I called at one?

B.   I was probably sitting outside in the sun.

A.   What were you doing when I called at four?

B.   I was painting the hallway and fixing the door.

A.   What were you doing when I called at six?

B.   I was washing the dog to get rid of his ticks.

A.   Well, I'm sorry I missed you when I tried to phone.

B.   It's too bad. I was there. I was home all alone.

G. NOBODY WANTS TO

| myself | yourself | himself | herself | ourselves | yourselves | themselves |

1. Nobody wants to go to the movies with me.

   I'll have to go to the movies by _____ *myself* _____.

2. Nobody wants to go to the baseball game with her.

   She'll have to go to the baseball game by _____.

3. Nobody wants to go bowling with us.

   We'll have to go bowling by _____.

4. Nobody wants to take a walk with you.

   You'll have to take a walk by _____.

5. Nobody wants to drive to the airport with them.

   They'll have to drive to the airport by _____.

6. Nobody wants to have dinner with him.

   He'll have to have dinner by _____.

7. Nobody wants to play cards with you and your brother.

   You'll have to play cards by _____.

H. WHAT'S THE WORD?

1. We were standing | on / into / over | the corner.

2. They were driving | out of / over / through | a bridge.

3. A can of paint fell | to / on / along | me.

4. Natasha always walks | to / under / along | work.

5. She was riding | in / along / through | an elevator.

6. Arthur likes to look | to / on / at | himself | on / in / at | the mirror.

7. Lois is afraid because she walked | through / over / under | a ladder.

8. Our children can cook breakfast themselves. | to / at / by |

89

I. WHAT HAPPENED?

bake	dance	shave	study
burn	have	skate	walk
cut	ride	sleep	

1. Alice hurt herself while _____*she was*_____ _____*skating*_____ .

2. I met my neighbor while _____ _____ home from work.

3. Sally saw a friend while _____ _____ her bicycle along Park Street.

4. Peter fell asleep while _____ _____ .

5. Bob stepped on Jane's feet while _____ _____ together.

6. I _____ myself while _____ _____ .

7. Mr. and Mrs. Brown _____ themselves while _____ _____ cookies.

8. Tommy _____ a nightmare while _____ at a friend's house.

J. RHYTHM: *By Themselves*

Listen. Then clap and practice.

A. Does she need a   ladder?   B.   No, she doesn't.

She can reach the top shelf by   herself.

All. She can reach the top shelf by   herself. Look at that!

She can reach the top shelf by   herself!

A. Does he need a   cart?   B.   No, he doesn't.

He can carry all the luggage by   himself.

All. He can carry all the luggage by   himself. Look at that!

He can carry all the luggage by   himself!

A. Do you need a   calculator?   B.   No, I don't.

I can add all these numbers by   myself.

All. You can add all those numbers by   yourself. Look at that!

You can add all those numbers by   yourself!

91

K. LOUD AND CLEAR

Fill in the words.   Then read the sentences aloud.

| eat | pieces | pizza | Rita | three |

1. _____*Rita*_____ is going to _____*eat*_____

_____*three*_____ _____*pieces*_____

of _____*pizza*_____ .

| delicious | didn't | dinner | finish |
| it | this | | |

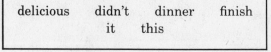

2. _____ _____ was

_____ , but we

_____ _____ _____ .

| Green | police | stealing | Street |
| thief | | | |

3. Call the _____! A _____

is _____ a car on

_____ _____ !

| busy | children | Ginger | is | office |
| Smith | with | | | |

4. _____ _____ sitting in

Doctor Smith's _____ _____

her sick _____ . Doctor

_____ is _____ .

| between | fifteen | leave | Rio |
| three | | | |

5. The plane to _____ is going to

_____ _____ three and

_____ _____ .

| big | building | city | in | is |
| live | sister | | | |

6. My _____ Hilda _____ going to

_____ _____ an apartment

_____ in a

_____ _____ .

A. WHAT'S THE WORD?

could   can
couldn't   can't

1. When I first arrived in this country, I was embarrassed because I _couldn't_ speak English.

   Now I'm happy because I _can_ speak English very well.

2. _____ Betty read when she was three years old?

   Yes, she _____ . She was very bright.

3. We _____ finish our dinner last night because we were too full.

4. My brother is very talented. He _____ speak three languages.

5. Lois _____ buy anything at the store because she didn't have any money.

6. When I was young, I _____ go dancing every night. I was very energetic.

7. Shirley is upset because her younger sister _____ sing beautifully, and she

   _____ .

8. _____ Stuart go to school yesterday?

   No, he _____ . He was too sick.

9. Mary _____ play on the basketball team when she was young because she was too short.

   But she wasn't upset because she _____ play on the baseball team.

10. Peter is a terrible dancer, but his little brother _____ dance very well.

11. George was very upset because he _____ go to the concert last night.

12. I'm glad you _____ go to the movies with us yesterday.

13. I really want to fire Larry, but I _____ . His father is president of the company.

Listen.　Then clap and practice.

A.　　She tried on the　skirt, but she　couldn't zip it　up.

B.　Was it too　small?

A.　　Much too　small.

A.　　She tried on the　shoes, but she　couldn't keep them on.

B.　Were they too　big?

A.　　Much too　big.

A.　　He tried to　talk, but he　couldn't say a　word.

B.　Was he too　nervous?

A.　　Much too　nervous.

A.　　She sat at the　table, but she　couldn't eat a　thing.

B.　Was she too　excited?

A.　　Much too　excited.

A.　　He went to the　lecture, but he　couldn't stay　awake.

B.　Was he too　tired?

A.　　Much too　tired.

A.　　She took the　course, but she　couldn't pass the　test.

B.　Was it too　hard?

A.　　Much too　hard.

C. YOU DECIDE: *Why Weren't They Able to?*

1. Anita _____*wasn't able to*_____ lift the package because _*it was too heavy* (or)_
    ....*she was too weak* (or) *she was too tired.*.......................

2. Tom and Harry _____ do their homework because ....
    ....

3. My brother _____ fall asleep last night because ....
    ....

4. Our cousins _____ go sailing yesterday because ....
    ....

5. Sally _____ wear her mother's shoes because ....
    ....

6. I _____ sit down on the train this morning because ....
    ....

7. My friends _____ eat any pizza last night because ....
    ....

8. Maria _____ drive a car last year because ....
    ....

9. We _____ walk home from the party last night because ....
    ....

10. Mr. and Mrs. Blake _____ buy the sofa they wanted
    because ....

11. John _____ get into my sports car last Friday because ....
    ....

D. WHEN THEY WERE YOUNG

could was/were able to	couldn't wasn't/weren't able to	had to

1. When I was young, I was angry because I $\begin{Bmatrix} couldn't \\ wasn't\ able\ to \end{Bmatrix}$ play with my friends after school.

   I _____ *had to* _____ get home early and take care of my little brother and sister.

2. When Janet was young, she wanted to watch TV after school every day, but she _____

   because she _____ do her homework.

3. Richard's teachers always gave him a lot of homework, and his parents _____
   help him because they were too busy.

4. Margaret's brother _____ go with her when she went out on dates
   because, in her mother's opinion, she was too young to go out by herself.

5. Nancy was upset because her older brothers _____ go to bed late, but

   she _____ . She _____ go to bed at 7:00 every evening.

6. When William was thirteen years old, his father got a job in Boston and the family moved

   there.   William was sad because he _____ see his old friends very
   often.

7. Roger was jealous of his rich friends because they _____ eat at fancy

   restaurants and they _____ buy expensive clothes.   He was embarrassed

   because he _____ wear his brother's old clothes.

8. Andrew was upset because he wanted to have long hair, but he _____ .   He

   _____ go to the barber every month because his parents liked short
   hair.

E. YOU DECIDE: *Why Didn't They Enjoy Themselves?*

myself	yourself	himself	herself	ourselves	yourselves	themselves

{ couldn't
  wasn't/weren't able to }

1. I didn't enjoy _____*myself*_____ at the beach yesterday.   It was very windy, and I

   ....*couldn't go swimming* (or) *wasn't able to go sailing.*..................................

2. Bobby and his friends didn't enjoy _____ in the park yesterday.   It was

   raining, and they ....

3. Susan didn't enjoy _____ at the restaurant yesterday.   She was very nervous

   about her examination, and she ....

4. George didn't enjoy _____ at the movies last night.   It was very crowded and

   noisy, and he ....

5. I didn't enjoy _____ at Gloria's party last Friday.   There were too many

   people there, and I ....

6. We didn't enjoy _____ on our vacation last winter.   We got sick and we

   ....

F. THEY'LL BE ABLE TO

couldn't	will be able to

1. Martha _____*couldn't*_____ find her shoes in the yard last night, but I'm sure _____*she'll be*_____

   _____*able to*_____ find them this morning.

2. We _____ move to our new apartment last month.   I hope _____

   _____ move there next month.

3. I _____ help Linda take care of her baby last week, but I think _____

   _____ help her this week.

4. Harry and Steve _____ go bowling with us last Friday, but I think _____

   _____ go bowling with us next week.

5. Roger _____ finish his homework last night, but I know _____

   _____ finish it tonight.

G. CARMEN

will/won't be able to

Carmen is a very energetic person.

1. She goes jogging every morning.
2. She rides her bicycle to school every day.
3. She plays soccer on the school team.
4. She swims every afternoon.
5. She does exercises every evening.

She's also very talented and capable.

6. She plays the guitar.
7. She writes her own songs.
8. She bakes delicious cakes and pies.
9. She makes her own clothes.

Last week Carmen went skiing, and unfortunately she broke her leg.   The doctor says she'll have to rest her leg all month.   Carmen is very upset.

1. _____ *She won't be able to go jogging every morning.* _____

2. _____

3. _____

4. _____

5. _____

Fortunately there are many things Carmen WILL be able to do.

6. _____ *She'll be able to play the guitar.* _____

7. _____

8. _____

9. _____

H. I'M SORRY

won't be able to	have/has got to

1. I'm really sorry. My husband and I _____won't be able to_____ go to the tennis match with you tomorrow. _____We've got to_____ take our son to the doctor.

2. I'm terribly sorry. My daughter _____ go to her ballet lesson this afternoon. _____ take care of her little brother.

3. I'm sorry. My children _____ go to the baseball game with you on Saturday. _____ study for an examination.

4. I'm really upset. My father _____ drive us to the beach tomorrow because _____ take my sister to the dentist.

5. I feel terrible. My wife and I _____ help you paint your apartment on Sunday. _____ visit our cousin in the hospital.

I. LISTEN

Listen to each story twice and then answer the questions you hear.

MR. AND MRS. SMITH'S VACATION

1. a. they were too busy.
   b. they were too old.
   c. the ocean was too cold.

2. a. better than today.
   b. worse than today.
   c. very cold.

3. a. they're too disappointed.
   b. they've got to leave early in the morning.
   c. the ocean will be cold.

HELEN'S ENGLISH EXAMINATION

4. a. English homework
   b. briefcase.
   c. glasses.

5. a. This morning.
   b. Last night.
   c. After the examination.

6. a. she got to school late.
   b. she did very well on her English examination.
   c. she didn't do well on her English examination.

99

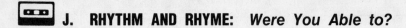

J. RHYTHM AND RHYME: *Were You Able to?*

Listen. Then clap and practice.

A. Were you able to · leave · early last · night?

B. No. I had to work until · seven. ·

A. Were you able to · get to the · office on · time?

B. No. I couldn't get there 'til · eleven. ·

A. Were you able to · take the · six o'clock · bus?

B. No. I had to wait until · eight. ·

A. Were you able to · get to the · meeting on · time?

B. No. I had to · walk in · late. ·

K. RHYTHM AND RHYME: *They Won't Be Able to*

Listen. Then clap and practice.

A. Will you be able to · help me · pack? ·

B. No, I · won't. I've · got to go · shopping. ·

A. Will he · able to · type this · letter? ·

B. No, he · won't. He's · got to call · Rome. ·

A. Will she be able to · meet us for · dinner? ·

B. No, she · won't. She's · got to work · late. ·

A. Will they be able to · stay for · lunch? ·

B. No, they · won't. They've · got to go · home. ·

100

CHECK-UP TEST: *Chapters 9–10*

A. Complete the sentences.

Ex. She (wash) _____*was washing*_____ her hair
when her boyfriend called.

1. We (paint) _____ the house
when it started to rain.

2. I (drive) _____ to work
when I got a flat tire.

3. They (study) _____
English when the lights went out.

4. Mary fell down while she (skate) _____

_____ .

5. John saw an accident while he (ride) _____

_____ his bicycle.

6. We met our neighbor while we (walk) _____

_____ home from work.

7. I cut myself while I (make) _____

_____ lunch.

B. Fill in the blanks.

Ex. I enjoyed _____*myself*_____ at the concert.

1. We didn't enjoy _____ at the
movies.

2. My father cut _____ while he
was shaving.

3. Did you and your wife enjoy

_____ at Robert's party?

4. Mr. and Mrs. Brown burned _____
while they were baking cookies.

5. Nobody went to the baseball game with
Judy.   She had to go to the baseball game

by _____ .

6. Did you fix the TV by _____ ,
or did your husband help you?

C. Put a circle around the correct word.

1. When I saw Tom, he was getting [on / off / into]
a taxi.

2. I usually get [at / up / off] the bus at Third Street.

3. When our teacher walked [out of / off / of] the
room, everybody started to talk.

4. We walked [in / into / out of] the nearest building
because it was raining.

5. Why were you getting [out of / off / from] a police car
at 8:00 this morning?

6. We [could / couldn't / can't] finish our dinner last night
because we were too full.

7. I'm sorry you [couldn't / can't / won't be able to] go to the
theater with us yesterday.

8. When Peter was young, he wanted to talk on
the telephone all afternoon, but he

[could / couldn't / had to] because he [could / couldn't / had to] do his
homework after school.

D. Fill in the blanks.

1. Bill _____ able to go to the beach yesterday because it was raining.

2. I'm glad you _____ able to go to the symphony with us last night.

3. Harry and Steve _____ able to walk home from the party last night because it was too dark.

4. I couldn't move to my new apartment last

   month, but I think _____ able to move there next month.

5. I feel terrible. I _____

   _____ able to go to your

   party tomorrow. _____ got to take my son to the doctor.

6. If you want to be the best violinist in your

   city, _____ got to practice.

7. I'm sorry. My daughter _____ able to go to her violin lesson next Monday.

   _____ got to study for an examination.

E. Listen to the story twice, and then answer the questions you hear.

POOR BILL!

1. a. happy.
    b. upset.
    c. generous.

2. a. got sick.
    b. saw an accident.
    c. got a flat tire.

3. a. his wife.
    b. the airport.
    c. a mechanic.

4. a. early.
    b. late.
    c. on time.

5. a. plane.
    b. train.
    c. bus.

A. GEORGE IS WORRIED ABOUT HIS HEALTH

less	fewer	more

George is worried about his health.   He always feels tired, and he doesn't know why.

In January he went to see Doctor Johnson.   Doctor Johnson thinks George feels tired because he eats too much salt.   According to Doctor Johnson, George must eat (−) _____fewer_____ potato chips, (−) _____ cheese, and (−) _____ salty crackers.   Also, he must eat (+) _____
2   3   4
fresh vegetables and (+) _____ rice.   George tried Doctor Johnson's diet, but it didn't
5
help.

In February George went to see Doctor Green.   Doctor Green thinks George feels tired because he's a little too thin.   According to Doctor Green, George must eat (−) _____ yogurt,
6
(−) _____ carrots, and (−) _____ celery.   Also, he must eat (+) _____
7   8   9
potatoes, (+) _____ spaghetti, and (+) _____ ice cream.   George tried
10   11
Doctor Johnson's diet, but it didn't help.

In March George went to see Doctor Wilson.   Doctor Wilson thinks George feels tired because he eats too much spicy food.   According to Doctor Wilson, George must eat (−) _____ garlic,
12
(−) _____ onions, and (−) _____ pizza.   Also, he must drink (+) _____
13   14   15
milk and (+) _____ water.   George tried Doctor Wilson's diet, but it didn't help.
16

In April George went to see Doctor Peterson.   Doctor Peterson thinks George feels tired because he eats too much sugar.   According to Doctor Peterson, George must eat (−) _____
17
cookies, (−) _____ ice cream, and (−) _____ cake.   Also, he must eat
18   19
(+) _____ meat and (+) _____ fish.   George tried Doctor Peterson's diet, but
20   21
it didn't help either.

Now George needs YOUR help.   What do YOU think?

George must eat/drink (−) ....
....
Also, he must eat/drink (+) ....
....

B. RHYTHM: *Diet Dilemma*

Listen.   Then clap and practice.

Candy,   cookies,   ice cream, cake!
Candy,   cookies,   ice cream, cake!
Eat less   candy!
Fewer   cookies!
Eat less   ice cream!
Eat less   cake!
Candy,   cookies,   ice cream, cake!
Candy,   cookies,   ice cream, cake!

Carrots,   beans,   grapefruit, greens!
Carrots,   beans,   grapefruit, greens!
Eat more   carrots!
Eat more   beans!
Eat more   grapefruit!
Eat more   greens!
Carrots,   beans,   grapefruit, greens!
Carrots,   beans,   grapefruit, greens!

C. THEY CAN'T WORK HERE

Mr. Smith

We didn't hire Miss Jones because she doesn't type accurately or speak Spanish.

1. If you want to work in Mr. Smith's office, you _____ *must type accurately*

_____ *and speak Spanish* .

Mrs. Norman

We fired Mr. Harris because he doesn't work quickly or dress neatly.

2. If you want to work in Mrs. Norman's office, you _____

_____ .

Miss Winter

We can't hire your cousin because he doesn't speak English or have a car.

3. If you want to work in Miss Winter's company, you _____

_____ .

Mrs. Nelson

We fired Mrs. Michaels because she isn't patient or kind.

4. If you want to teach in Mrs. Nelson's school, you _____

_____ .

Mr. Jackson

We can't hire Fifi because she doesn't act, sing, or dance very well.

5. If you want to act in Mr. Jackson's play, you _____

_____ .

D. TWO VERY DIFFERENT SCHOOLS

Fill in the blanks with the most appropriate words.

> must
> mustn't
> don't have to

Miss Primm's School and the Flower School are very different.

At Miss Primm's you _____*must*_____ get to school on time every morning. If you're late,
₁

your parents _____ write a letter to the teacher.
₂

At the Flower School you _____ get to school on time. If you're a few minutes late,
₃

the teachers aren't upset.

At Miss Primm's School the boys _____ wear jackets and ties every day, and the girls
₄

_____ wear dresses or skirts. Some girls at Miss Primm's want to wear pants to school, but
₅

Miss Primm says they _____ .
₆

At the Flower School students can wear any clothes they like, but they _____ dress
₇

neatly. The boys are happy because they _____ wear jackets and ties every day, and the
₈

girls are happy because they can wear pants.

At Miss Primm's School you _____ have a notebook for every subject, and you
₉

_____ forget to take your notebooks to class. Also, at Miss Primm's you _____
₁₀ ₁₁

be VERY quiet while you're working.

At the Flower School you can talk to your friends, but you ＿＿＿＿＿ talk too loudly.
12

At Miss Primm's School you ＿＿＿＿＿ stand and say "hello" very politely when a teacher
13
walks into the room.

At the Flower School you ＿＿＿＿＿ stand when a teacher walks into the room.   You can
14
sit and work, and nobody thinks you're impolite.

At Miss Primm's School you ＿＿＿＿＿ always agree with your teacher because, according
15
to Miss Primm, the teacher is always right.

At the Flower School you ＿＿＿＿＿ agree with your teacher all the time.   If you
16
have a different opinion, your teacher will be glad to listen.

E. WRITE ABOUT YOUR SCHOOL

At our school you must ....

You mustn't ....

You don't have to ....

F. YOU DECIDE: *What Did They Say?*

```
┌─────────────────────────────┐
│  must        mustn't        │
└─────────────────────────────┘
```

1. I talked to my doctor and she told me ....

.... because I'm too heavy.

2. Mary talked to her doctor and he told her ....

.... because she's too thin.

3. Jack talked to his English teacher and she told him ....

.... because he makes too many mistakes.

4. I talked to the vet and he told me my dog ....

.... because he's always sick.

5. Betty talked to the doctor and he told her ....

.... because she's too nervous.

6. We talked to our landlord and he told us ....

.... because the neighbors are upset.

G. THE CHECKUP

blood	clothes	heart	pressure
blood test	examination	hospital gown	pulse
chest	examination room	measure	scale
			weight

1. Please go into the _____.

2. Please take off your _____ and put on this _____.

3. Please stand on this _____ so I can _____ your height

   and your _____.

4. Did the nurse take your _____?

5. Now I want to listen to your _____.

6. I have to draw some _____ for a _____.

7. We should probably take a _____ X-ray.

8. I'm worried about your blood _____.

9. I think you should have a complete _____ every year.

H. SCRAMBLED MEDICAL WORDS

Unscramble the words.

1. midragorca _____

2. sheepcostot _____

3. stech _____

4. slupe _____

5. sersepru _____

6. maxinee _____

I. LOUD AND CLEAR

Fill in the words. **Then read the sentences aloud.**

Helen	her	hire

1. Should I _____*hire*_____ _____*Helen*_____

   or _____*her*_____ sister?

hamburger	hungry	who	whole

2. Who's _____? _____

   wants a _____ on

   _____ wheat bread?

Harry	head	hockey	hurt

3. _____ _____ his

   _____ at the _____

   game.

healthy	her	Hilda	husband

4. _____ and _____

   _____ are _____

   and happy.

half	Henry	his	homework
	hopes		

5. _____ _____ he'll

   finish _____ _____

   in an hour and a _____ .

happy	Hawaii	hello	here
	Honolulu		

6. _____! We're _____

   you're _____ in _____,

   _____ .

J. RHYTHM AND INTONATION: *Advice*

Listen. Then clap and practice.

A. You must slow   down.
    You're working too   hard.

B. Me? Slow   down?   Don't be   silly!

A. You must eat less   candy.
    You're a little   overweight.

B. Me? Eat less   candy?   Don't be   silly!

A. You must learn to   swim.
    It's good for your   back.

B. Me? Learn to   swim?   Don't be   silly!

A. You must take it   easy.
    You look very   tired.

B. Me? Take it   easy?   Don't be   silly!

K. RHYTHM AND RHYME: *You Must . . .*

Listen. Then clap and practice.

A. You must clean your room.

B. But I cleaned it on   Sunday!

A. You must do the   laundry.

B. But I did it last   Monday!

A. You must fix the   fence.

B. But I fixed it in   June!

A. You must do your   homework.

B. I'll finish it   soon!

A. THEY'LL ALL BE BUSY

1. Will Mr. and Mrs. Jones be busy this afternoon?

   Yes, they will.   They'll

   be painting their kitchen.

2. Will Peggy be busy this morning?

   _____

   _____

3. Will you and your wife be busy today?

   _____

   _____

4. Will George and Martha be busy tomorrow morning?

   _____

   _____

5. Will you be busy this Saturday?

   _____

   _____

6. Will your children be busy after school today?

   _____

   _____

7. Will Miss Smith be busy this morning?

   _____

   _____

8. Will Sally be busy this afternoon?

   _____

   _____

B. ARTHUR TRIES AGAIN

Arthur was upset after he talked to Gloria.   He decided to call Louise.

A. Hi, Louise.   This is Arthur.
Can I come over and visit this afternoon?

B. No, Arthur.   I'm afraid I won't be home

this afternoon.   I'll be ....

....

A. I see.   Can I come over and visit TOMORROW
afternoon?

B. No, Arthur.   I'm afraid I won't be home

tomorrow afternoon.   I'll be ....

....

A. Oh.   Can I come over and visit this WEEKEND?

B. No, Arthur.   I'll be ....

....

A. Well, can I come over and visit next Tuesday?

B. No, Arthur.   I'll be ....

....

A. How about some time next SUMMER?

B. No, Arthur.   I'll be getting married next
summer.

A. Oh, no!   Not again!!

Listen. Then clap and practice.

A. What do you think you'll be doing next spring?

B. I'll probably be doing the same old thing.

A. What do you think he'll be doing this fall?

B. I'm sure he'll be working downtown at the mall.

A. When do you think they'll be leaving for Spain?

B. I think they'll be taking the four o'clock plane.

A. When do you think you'll be hearing from Anne?

B. I'm sure she'll be calling as soon as she can.

A. When do you think we'll be hearing from Jack?

B. I'm sure he'll be phoning as soon as he's back.

A. What do you think she'll be doing at two?

B. I think she'll be taking the kids to the zoo.

A. Where do you think they'll be living next year?

B. As far as we know, they'll be living right here.

D. UNTIL WHEN?

1. How much longer will you be working at the bank?

_____ *I'll be working* _____ at the bank | for / in / (until) | September.

2. How late will Peter be reading tonight?

_____ | at / in / until | 11:30.

3. How much longer will Gladys be practicing the violin?

_____ the violin | for / in / until | a few more hours.

4. Where will they be getting on the bus?

_____ on the bus | at / for / in | State Street.

5. How much longer will Richard be playing tennis?

_____ tennis | at / for / until | he gets tired.

6. Where will you be getting off the train?

_____ the train | at / in / until | the next stop.

7. How much longer will we be waiting for the plane?

_____ the plane | at / for / until | 15 more minutes.

114

8.

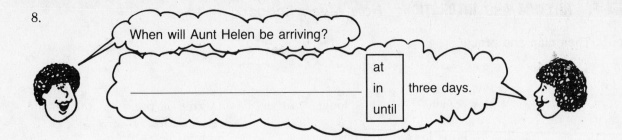

When will Aunt Helen be arriving?

_____
| at |
| in | three days.
| until |

E. WHAT'S THE QUESTION?

1.

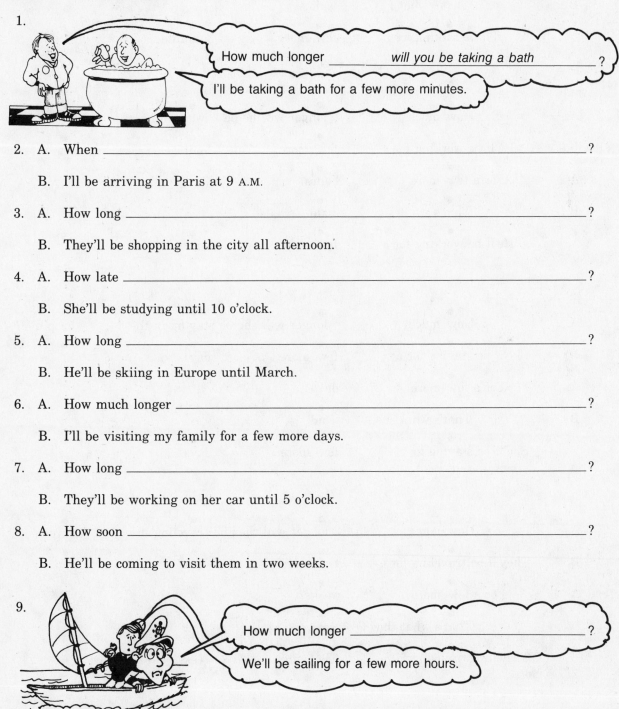

How much longer _____ *will you be taking a bath* ?

I'll be taking a bath for a few more minutes.

2. A. When _____ ?

   B. I'll be arriving in Paris at 9 A.M.

3. A. How long _____ ?

   B. They'll be shopping in the city all afternoon.

4. A. How late _____ ?

   B. She'll be studying until 10 o'clock.

5. A. How long _____ ?

   B. He'll be skiing in Europe until March.

6. A. How much longer _____ ?

   B. I'll be visiting my family for a few more days.

7. A. How long _____ ?

   B. They'll be working on her car until 5 o'clock.

8. A. How soon _____ ?

   B. He'll be coming to visit them in two weeks.

9.

How much longer _____ ?

We'll be sailing for a few more hours.

F. RHYTHM AND INTONATION: *How Much Longer?*

Listen. Then clap and practice.

A. How much   longer will you be   talking on the   telephone?

B. I'll be talking for a   few more   minutes.

A. For a few more   minutes?

B. That's what I   said.

    I'll be talking for a   few more   minutes.

A. How much   longer will he be   working?

B. He'll be working for a   few more   hours.

A. For a few more   hours?

B. That's what he   said.

    He'll be working for a   few more   hours.

A. How much   longer will she be staying in the   hospital?

B. She'll be staying for a   few more   days.

A. For a few more   days?

B. That's what she   said.

    She'll be staying for a   few more   days.

A. How much   longer will they be traveling in   Europe?

B. They'll be traveling for a   few more   weeks.

A. For a few more   weeks?

B. That's what they   said.

    They'll be traveling for a   few more   weeks.

116

G. WHY DON'T YOU . . . . ?

1. A. Why don't you call Billy before dinner?

   B. I don't want to disturb him. I'm sure _____*he'll be*_____ _____*practicing the piano*_____. He always *practices* _____*the piano*_____ before dinner.

2. A. Why don't you visit your brother-in-law this morning?

   B. I don't want to disturb him. I'm sure _____ _____. He always _____ _____ on Saturday morning.

3. A. Why don't you call Sally this evening?

   B. I don't want to disturb her. I'm sure _____ _____. She _____ _____ every evening.

4. A. Why don't you call William after school?

   B. I don't want to disturb him. I'm sure _____ _____. He _____ _____ every day after school.

5. A. Why don't you visit Carol and Dan tonight?

   B. I don't want to disturb them. I'm sure _____ _____. They usually _____ _____ on Thursday night.

(continued)

6. A. Why don't you call Jane after breakfast?

    B. I don't want to disturb her. I'm sure _____

    _____. She _____

    _____ every day after breakfast.

7. A. Why don't you visit Barbara this afternoon?

    B. I don't want to disturb her. I'm sure _____

    _____. She usually _____

    _____ on Saturday afternoon.

H. LISTEN

Listen and fill in the blanks with the words you hear.

ON THE AIRPLANE

Good afternoon. This is Captain Harris speaking. Our plane ____*will be*____ leaving
                                                                    1
in just a few minutes. Soon ____*we'll be*____ flying over New York City, and _____
                                2
_____ to see the baseball stadium on your _____
              3   4
and Central Park on your _____. We'll be flying _____ the
                                  5   6
Atlantic Ocean _____ three and a half hours. _____, you'll
                      7   8
be _____ dinner, and after dinner _____ a movie.
          9   10
_____ in San Juan at 8:35. The weather in San Juan
                  11
this evening is 70°F./21°C. and cloudy. _____ probably _____
                                                12   13
when we get there.

118

IN THE HOSPITAL

Now Mr. Jones, after your operation, _____ probably _____
1
_____ weak _____. But don't worry! _____
2   3
_____ good care of you.   Tomorrow _____
4
_____ in bed and resting _____ all day.   The nurses _____
5   6
_____ your pulse and _____ pressure, and _____
7   8
_____ you _____ soup and juice.   The day after tomorrow
9   10
_____ and _____ eat ice cream and yogurt.   If
11   12
everything _____ okay, _____ the hospital on Saturday.   Do you
13   14
have _____ questions?
15

YOU'LL FIND ME

When you come _____ the restaurant, _____ who I am. _____
1   2
_____ dark glasses and a raincoat. _____ by myself
3   4
at a table _____, and _____ a glass of
5   6
water and _____ a newspaper.   And _____ for
7   8
you. _____ me.   Don't worry!
9   10

119

A. HELP

13

me	him	her	us	you	them
my	his	her	our	your	their
myself	himself	herself	ourselves	yourself	themselves
				yourselves	

1. ___*His*___ family didn't help

___*him*___. He washed the kitchen

floor by ___*himself*___.

2. _____ mother didn't help

_____. They baked this delicious

bread by _____.

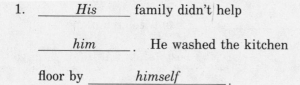

3. _____ parents usually help

_____. But yesterday she studied

by _____.

4. _____ friends can't help

_____. We've got to paint the

kitchen by _____.

5. Nobody is going to help _____.

He has to fix _____ car by

_____.

6. I wrote this letter by _____.

I'm glad _____ parents didn't help

_____.

7. You don't have to paint the bathroom

by _____ . I really

want to help _____ .

8. Do you have any questions?

I'll be glad to help _____ . You

don't have to do _____ homework

by _____ .

B. THE LOST UMBRELLA

mine	ours
his	yours
hers	theirs

A. I just found this umbrella in the closet. Is it ___*yours*___?
   $\overline{}_{1}$

B. No. It isn't _____ . But it might be your friend Mary's. She always forgets things.
   $_{2}$

A. No. I'm sure it isn't _____ . Her umbrella is red, and this one is polka dot.
   $_{3}$

B. Do you think it might be Jeff's?

A. Jeff's?! No. It can't be _____ . He doesn't have a polka dot umbrella!
   $_{4}$

B. How about Judy and Steve? Do you think it might be _____ ?
   $_{5}$

A. Not really. When they forget something, they always call right away.

B. Well, I don't know WHO forgot this umbrella, but WE certainly need one.

A. You're right. And if nobody asks for it soon, I guess it'll be _____ !
   $_{6}$

C. SCRAMBLED SENTENCES   Unscramble the sentences.

1. when   sister   going   her   their   is   to   visit?

   _____ _____ _____ _____ _____

   _____ _____ _____

2. are   brown   yours   these   gloves?

   _____ _____ _____

3. he   give   wants   to   his   her   book

_____ _____ _____ _____ _____

_____ _____

4. we   send   her   him   address   didn't

_____ _____ _____ _____ _____

5. we   ourselves   us   because   enjoyed   friends   our   with   were

_____ _____ _____ _____ _____

_____ _____

6. he   dinner   cooks   his   by   because   help   himself   children don't   him

_____ _____ _____ _____ _____

_____ _____ _____ _____

7. they're   father's   writing   pen   their   with   because   theirs they   lost

_____ _____ _____ _____

_____ _____ _____ _____

D. NOISY NEIGHBORS

It's 4 A.M., and Michael can't fall asleep because his [neighbors / (neighbor's)]¹ daughter [is playing / will be playing]²

the piano. Last night she [played / is playing]³ the piano [until / for]⁴ six hours, and Michael [won't be / wasn't]⁵

able to [fall / fell]⁶ asleep. He's very upset because he studies [hardly / hard]⁷ all day and needs to sleep

[at / in the]⁸ night. He doesn't know what to do.

122

It's midnight, and I'm not asleep because the boy [upstairs / downstairs]9 is lifting [heights / weights]10. I don't

know why he isn't [quietly / quieter]11! I don't like [complain / to complain]12, but if that boy [lifts / won't lift]13 weights

again tomorrow night, I think I'll talk [to / at]14 the landlord or maybe even call the police!

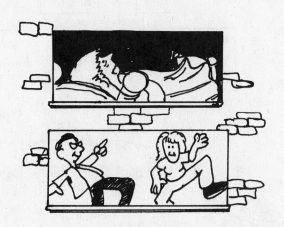

It's 2 A.M., and Helen can't fall asleep because [her / hers]15 downstairs neighbors [were dancing / are dancing]16.

Last night they [dance / danced]17 [for / until]18 3 A.M., and Helen is afraid that they [might / should]19 dance all night

tonight! The music is very [loud / loudly]20, and Helen's neighbors are very [noisy / noisily]21 dancers. Helen is

upset. She doesn't like to complain, but she also doesn't like [too tired / to be tired]22 every morning. She

doesn't know what to do.

(continued)   123

It's 2 A.M., and [I practice / I'm practicing]²³ the violin. I study music [in / during]²⁴ the day at music school.

After school I work in a restaurant [until / for]²⁵ 9 o'clock. When I get home, [I'm eating / I eat]²⁶ dinner and

sleep for [a few / a little]²⁷ hours because I'm usually very tired. Then I get up at midnight and start to

practice the violin. My music teacher [says / tells]²⁸ me I [have to / had to]²⁹ practice [for / until]³⁰ four hours every

day. If I [don't / won't]³¹ practice, I [wasn't / won't be]³² able to play the violin [well / good]³³. I try to play [quiet / quietly]³⁴.

I hope my neighbors are able to sleep.

E. WHAT'S THE WORD?

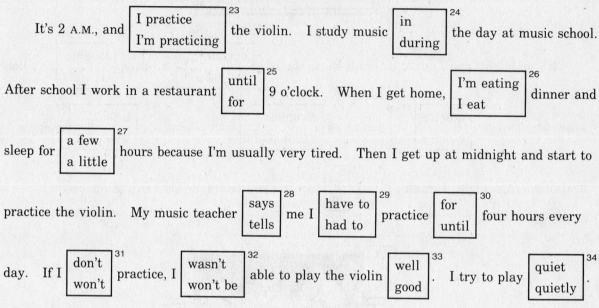

1. I don't like Richard. He never says [anyone / (anything)] nice about [anybody / nobody].

You're right. [Anybody / Nobody] likes him.

2. A. There's [anything / something] wrong with my car.

B. Is there [anyone / anything] I can do to help?

A. No. I'm afraid [nobody / somebody] can help me. I've got to fix it myself.

124

3. A. Look! [Anybody / Somebody] ate all the ice cream!

   B. That's terrible! [Anybody / Nobody] will be able to have it for dessert tonight.

4. A. I went over to Alice's house, but [nobody / somebody] was home.

   B. I know. [Everyone / Someone] in the family is on vacation.

5. A. There's [anybody / somebody] in the yard. Who do you think it is?

   B. I don't have [any / some] idea.

6. A. I'm hungry. Is there [anything / everything] to eat?

   B. No. There isn't [anything / something] in the refrigerator.

7. A. [Anybody / Somebody] took Ellen's briefcase at school this morning.

   B. I know. And [anybody / nobody] knows who did it.

   A. Do you think it was [nobody / anybody] in our class?

   B. Of course not. [Everybody / Somebody] in our class is honest.

▣ F. LISTEN: *The School Picnic*

Listen and put a circle around the correct answer.

1. a. No. We won't be able to go.

   b. No. I didn't enjoy myself very much.

   c. I don't know. My watch was broken.

2. a. No. I forgot to take a good book.

   b. Yes. She ate everything.

   c. The food was okay, but I wasn't hungry.

3. a. At 12:00.

   b. Until 12:30.

   c. In a few hours.

4. a. Because I was cleaning
        the apartment.

    b. Because I had to go
        home and take care of
        my younger brother.

    c. Because I won't be able
        to take my sister to
        the doctor.

5. a. I hope it was.

    b. I'm sure it is.

    c. We'll just have to wait
        and see.

G. YOU DECIDE: *What's Mr. Smith Saying?*

A. Hello.   May I speak to Mr. Smith?

B. ....

A. There's something wrong with my TV, and I need a TV repair person who can come over
    and fix it.

B. ....

A. No.   It's a black-and-white TV.

B. ....

A. I don't know what's wrong.   It just doesn't work at all.

B. ....

A. I live at 156 Grove Street in Centerville.

B. ....

A. Drive down State Street and turn left.   My house is the last one on the right.

B. ....

A. Not really.   I'm afraid I won't be home tomorrow at 2:00.   Can you come down at any
    other time?

B. ....

A. That's fine.   I'll see you then.

B. Good-bye.

A. Good-bye.

H. RHYTHM: *I Clean It Myself*

Listen. Then clap and practice.

A. Who cleans your   house?
B. I clean it   myself.
A. Does your wife   help you?
B. She helps me if I   ask her.

A. Who does your   laundry?
B. I do it   myself.
A. Does your husband   help you?
B. He helps me if I   ask him.

A. Who washes the   dishes?
B. He washes them himself.
A. Does his daughter   help him?
B. She helps him if he   asks her.

A. Who fixes   breakfast?
B. She fixes it   herself.
A. Does her father   help her?
B. He helps her if she   asks him.

A. Who does your   shopping?
B. We do it   ourselves.
A. Do your children   help you?
B. They help us if we   ask them.

A. Who does their   homework?
B. They do it   themselves.
A. Does their mother   help them?
B. She helps them if they ask her.

I. YOU DECIDE: *Why Can't They Go to the Movies?*

A.   Would you like to go to the movies with me this afternoon?

B.   ....

A.   That's too bad.   Do you think Jack might be able to go?

B.   ....

A.   That's right.   I forgot.   He's always busy on Friday afternoon.   How about Alice and Jane?   They usually like to go to the movies.

B.   ....

A.   Well, I hope they enjoy themselves.   Do you think Sally might want to go?

B.   ....

A.   Poor Sally.   She always has problems with her house.   How about Ted?

B.   ....

A.   Really?   That's terrible.   Nobody told me!   How did it happen?

B.   ....

A.   When you see him, tell him I'm very sorry.   Well, I guess I won't go to the movies tonight.   Maybe I'll stay home and study.

J. WHAT'S THE  WORD?

Put a circle around the correct word.

1.   Last he was too to get out of bed.

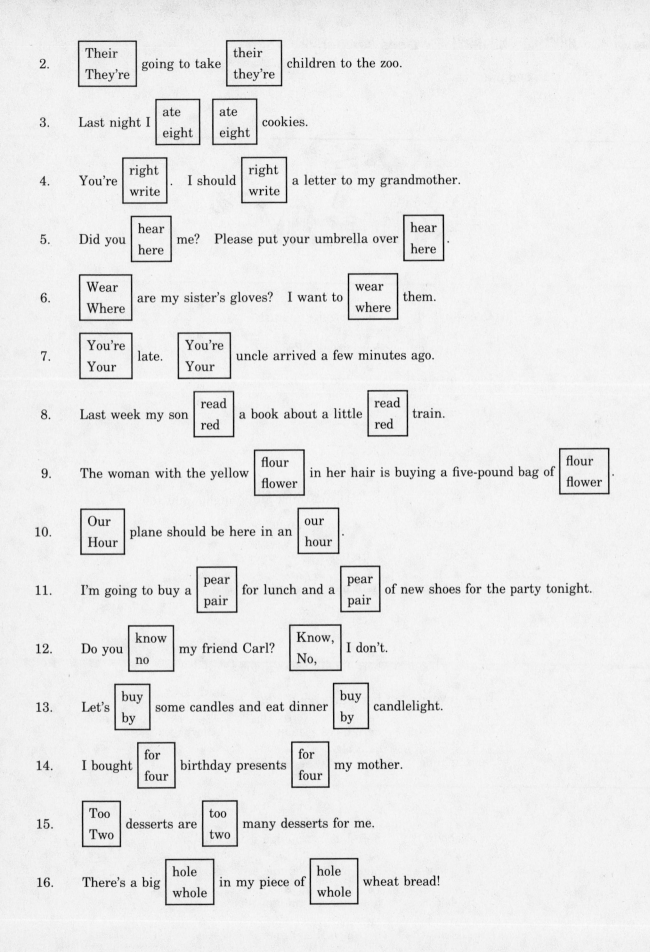

2. | Their / They're | going to take | their / they're | children to the zoo.

3. Last night I | ate / eight | | ate / eight | cookies.

4. You're | right / write | . I should | right / write | a letter to my grandmother.

5. Did you | hear / here | me? Please put your umbrella over | hear / here | .

6. | Wear / Where | are my sister's gloves? I want to | wear / where | them.

7. | You're / Your | late. | You're / Your | uncle arrived a few minutes ago.

8. Last week my son | read / red | a book about a little | read / red | train.

9. The woman with the yellow | flour / flower | in her hair is buying a five-pound bag of | flour / flower | .

10. | Our / Hour | plane should be here in an | our / hour | .

11. I'm going to buy a | pear / pair | for lunch and a | pear / pair | of new shoes for the party tonight.

12. Do you | know / no | my friend Carl? | Know, / No, | I don't.

13. Let's | buy / by | some candles and eat dinner | buy / by | candlelight.

14. I bought | for / four | birthday presents | for / four | my mother.

15. | Too / Two | desserts are | too / two | many desserts for me.

16. There's a big | hole / whole | in my piece of | hole / whole | wheat bread!

129

K. RHYTHM AND RHYME: *Does Anybody?*

Listen.   Then clap and practice.

Does anybody here speak Spanish?

Does anybody here speak French?

Does anyone here have a hammer?

Does anyone here have a wrench?

Somebody here speaks Spanish.

Somebody here speaks French.

Someone here has a hammer.

Someone here has a wrench.

Does anybody here have change for a dollar?

Does anyone here have a dime?

Does anybody here have a map of the city?

Does anyone here have the time?

Nobody here has change for a dollar.

Nobody here has a dime.

Nobody here has a map of the city.

Nobody here has the time.

CHECK-UP TEST: *Chapters 11–13*

A. Complete the sentences.

Ex. Will you be home this evening?
Yes, I will. (watch TV)

_____ *I'll be watching TV* _____ .

1. Will your parents be busy this afternoon?
Yes, they will. (paint)

_____ the garage.

2. Will your sister be home at 4:00?
Yes, she will. (study)

_____

3. Will your brother be home at 5:00?
Yes, he will. (practice)

_____ the piano.

4. Will you and your wife be busy this
afternoon?
Yes, we will. (take care of)

_____ our
grandchildren.

5. Will you be at the office tonight?
Yes, I will. (work)

_____ late.

B. Complete the questions.

Ex. When _____ *will you be getting married* _____ ?
We'll be getting married next summer.

1. How late _____

_____?
She'll be working until 8:00.

2. How much longer _____

_____?
I'll be reading for a few more hours.

3. How soon _____

_____?
He'll be coming tomorrow morning.

4. How far _____

_____?
They'll be driving until they reach Tokyo.

5. How long _____

_____?
We'll be staying in New York until Sunday.

C. Put a circle around the correct answer.

1. My doctor says I must eat | less / fewer | butter,

| less / fewer | eggs, and | less / fewer | fatty meat.

2. I | mustn't / don't have to | study tonight, but I think
I should.

3. Mary | mustn't / doesn't have to | eat too | much / many |

salt because she has problems with her
blood pressure.

4. If you want to get a job in Mr. Wilson's office,
you must speak English and Spanish, but you

| mustn't / don't have to | type very well.

5. We'll be working at the bank | for / until |
September.

6. She'll be playing the violin | for / until | a few
more minutes.

7. We finished our dinner | at / until | 6:00.

8. I'll be going to Paris | at / in | a few days.

9. I have to go to the supermarket. There isn't

| anything / something | in the refrigerator.

(continued)   131

10. If you look in the yellow pages, I'm sure

you'll find [anybody / somebody] who can fix your TV.

11. [Anyone / Someone] ate all the yogurt in the refrigerator.

12. This is his sandwich. It isn't [my / mine].

13. I don't think this is [their / theirs] book, but it

might be [her / hers].

14. We gave [her / his] our address.

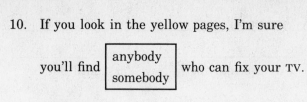 D. **Listen and fill in the missing words.**

ON THE BUS

Good morning. This is your bus driver, Jim Smith, speaking. I'm glad

_____ with us on this
₁

special weekend visit to New York City.

_____ in just a few minutes
₂

and _____ in New York City
₃

at noon, in time for a delicious lunch at the Park Avenue Cafe. After lunch

_____ the United Nations,
₄

and in the evening _____
₅

dinner at one of New York's finest restaurants.

Don't forget! _____ at the
₆

Fifth Avenue Hotel across the street from the beautiful Museum of Modern Art. I'm sure

you're all going to enjoy _____
₇

very much. If I can do _____
₈

to help you, _____

_____ .
₉

132

TAPE SCRIPTS FOR LISTENING EXERCISES

Page 9   Exercise K

John is busy this month.

On July 2nd he's going bowling.
On July 4th he's going to a concert.
On July 8th he's going to the dentist.
On July 11th he's going sailing.
On July 16th he's going to a football game.
On July 20th he's going to a party.
On July 27th he's going swimming.
On July 29th he's going to the doctor.
On July 31st he's going to a wedding.

Page 9   Exercise L

Many people live and work in this building in New York City.
1. Peter Jones lives in an apartment on the 4th floor.
2. The Smith Family lives in an apartment on the 14th floor.
3. The PRESTO Company has an office on the 19th floor.
4. Mary Nelson works in an office on the 7th floor.
5. There's a drug store on the 1st floor.
6. There's a dentist's office on the 35th floor.
7. Barbara Harris and her son live on the 30th floor.
8. Mr. and Mrs. Brown live in an apartment on the 13th floor.
9. Dr. Johnson has an office on the 28th floor.
10. Mr. Jackson works in an office on the 10th floor.
11. Hilda Green lives in a small apartment on the 46th floor.
12. There's a flower shop on the 2nd floor.
13. Dr. Rinaldi has an office on the 15th floor.
14. The Larson family lives on the 41st floor.
15. Mrs. Nathan has an office on the 12th floor.
16. There's a French restaurant on the 50th floor.

Page 14   Exercise D

1. May I have some milk?
2. I'm looking for some tomatoes.
3. I'm looking for some bread.
4. I want some eggs.
5. I want some lettuce.
6. Let's have some chicken!
7. May I have some beans?
8. I'm looking for some mayonnaise.
9. May I have some flour?
10. I'm looking for some crackers.
11. I want some cheese.
12. Let's have some rice!
13. I want some pears.
14. May I have some soda?
15. I'm looking for some onions.
16. May I have some orange juice?

Page 19   Exercise I

1. A. Would you care for some more?
   B. Yes, please.   But not too many.
2. I like it, but it's bad for my health.
3. My doctor says they're good for my health.
4. A. These are really delicious.
   B. I'm glad you like them.
5. A. How many did you eat?
   B. I ate so many that I have a stomachache.
6. I bought it this morning, and it's very fresh. Would you care for a little?

Page 23   Exercise B

1. A bunch of carrots costs 55¢.
2. A bag of potatoes costs $1.80.
3. A box of cereal costs $2.15.
4. A bunch of bananas costs 95¢.
5. A loaf of bread costs 99¢.
6. A pound of cheese costs $2.98.
7. A quart of milk costs 89¢.
8. A pound of butter costs $1.73.
9. A bag of onions costs $1.19.
10. A can of vegetable soup costs 67¢.
11. A box of cookies costs $1.30.
12. A bag of flour costs $1.20.

Page 27   Exercise F

1. David usually has two bowls of cereal for breakfast.   This morning he got up late and had a glass of milk.
2. Jane usually has a glass of orange juice with her lunch.   Yesterday, she had two glasses of milk.
3. Mr. Nelson usually has two cups of coffee with his dinner.   Yesterday he visited his Japanese neighbors and had a cup of tea.
4. Peter usually has a bowl of soup for lunch. Yesterday he was very hungry, and he had three pieces of chicken.
5. Lois usually has a dish of yogurt for lunch.   This afternoon she went to a restaurant and had two orders of french fries.
6. Marie usually has a piece of cheese for dessert. Yesterday she went to a party and had three dishes of ice cream.
7. Alice usually has a cup of hot chocolate for breakfast. Yesterday morning she went to a restaurant and had an order of pancakes.
8. Nancy usually has a piece of cake for dessert. Yesterday she visited her grandmother and had two pieces of pie and a bowl of strawberries.

Page 31   Exercise E

Ex.   I'm looking for some milk.

1.   I'm looking for some crackers.
2.   May I have some flour?
3.   Let's have some cheese!
4.   I want some eggs.
5.   May I have some orange juice?

Page 34   Exercise D

1.   I want to visit my cousin.
2.   I won't visit my uncle.
3.   We won't write to our sister.
4.   We want to go to New York.
5.   Peter and John won't go home.
6.   They want to call their mother.
7.   I want to walk to school.
8.   Dan won't take the bus.
9.   My mother and father want to live in Athens.
10.   I won't drive your new car.
11.   I want to eat a big dinner.
12.   We want to get up at 7:00.
13.   She won't wear her new blouse.
14.   They won't get married soon.
15.   They want to get married soon.

Page 47   Exercise I

1.   George is noisier than Jennifer.
2.   Albert is richer than John.
3.   Ted's dog is bigger than Fred and Sally's dog.
4.   Robert is happier than Nancy.
5.   Edward's English test was more difficult than his French test.
6.   Margaret is older than Alice.
7.   Eggs are cheaper than bread this week.
8.   Bob is shorter and heavier than Bill.

Page 63   Exercise G

Ex.   Alice is younger than Margaret.

1.   Bob is taller than Bill.
2.   Tea is more expensive than champagne.
3.   David is heavier than Herman.
4.   Stockholm is colder than Madrid.
5.   Carl's homework is more difficult than Jack's homework.

Page 71   Exercise H

1.   John was at the restaurant on Maple Street.   He walked up Maple Street to Grand Avenue and turned left.   He walked along Grand Avenue to the building next to the post office.   Where did he go?
2.   Helen was at the shoe store on Brighton Boulevard. She walked along Brighton Boulevard to Elm Street and turned left.   She walked up Elm Street to the building next to the Bellview Hotel.   Where did she go?
3.   Mr. and Mrs. Larson were at the motel on Elm Street. They walked down Elm Street to Brighton Boulevard and turned right.   They walked along Brighton Boulevard to the building across from the museum. Where did they go?
4.   Tommy was at the candy store on Maple Street.   He walked up Maple Street to Grand Avenue and turned right.   He walked along Grand Avenue to the building between the newsstand and the butcher shop.   Where did he go?

5.   Julie was at the university on Brighton Boulevard. She walked along Brighton Boulevard to Maple Street and turned left.   She walked up Maple Street to Grand Avenue and turned right.   She walked along Grand Avenue to the building across from the pet shop.   Where did she go?
6.   Peggy and Paul were at the supermarket on Maple Street.   They walked up Maple Street to Brighton Boulevard and turned right.   They walked along Brighton Boulevard to Elm Street and turned left. They walked up Elm Street to the building next to the flower shop.   Where did they go?
7.   Mrs. Wilson and her son were at the laundromat on Brighton Boulevard.   They walked along Brighton Boulevard to Maple Street and turned right.   They walked up Maple Street to the building next to the restaurant at the corner of Maple Street and Grand Avenue.   Where did they go?

Page 73   Exercise C

1.   He isn't a sloppy painter.   He's very _____.
2.   I can't read their homework because they write very _____.
3.   David never makes mistakes.   He's very _____.
4.   At the concert last night Antonio played the piano _____.
5.   I don't dance very well because I'm not _____
6.   She isn't a good tennis player.   She plays tennis very _____.
7.   Your homework is very interesting, but it's _____.
8.   Mr. and Mrs. Smith always dress _____.
9.   Leave the party early and drive home _____.
10.   She's a good worker, but she's _____.
11.   Mary skated carelessly yesterday.   That's strange.   She's usually _____.
12.   Ted does his homework _____.

Page 83   Exercise F

1.   Mrs. Johnson was at the park on Park Street.   She walked up Park Street to Third Avenue and turned right.   She walked along Third Avenue to the building between the pet shop and the post office. Where did she go?
2.   Arthur was at the TV station on River Street.   He walked down River Street to Second Avenue and turned right.   He walked along Second Avenue to the building across from the beauty parlor.   Where did he go?
3.   Mr. and Mrs. Schultz were at the supermarket on Second Avenue.   They walked along Second Avenue to Park Street and turned left.   They walked up Park Street to Third Avenue and turned right. They walked along Third Avenue to the building across from the motel.   Where did they go?
4.   Frieda was at the zoo on Third Avenue.   She walked along Third Avenue to Park Street and turned right. She walked down Park Street to Second Avenue and turned left.   She walked along Second Avenue to the building next to the beauty parlor.   Where did she go?

5. Mr. and Mrs. Williams were at the hotel on Park Street. They walked up Park Street to Second Avenue and turned right. They walked along Second Avenue to River Street and turned left. They walked up River Street to the building next to the TV station, at the corner of River Street and Third Avenue. Where did they go?

Page 99 Exercise I

MR. AND MRS. SMITH'S VACATION

Mr. and Mrs. Smith aren't enjoying their vacation at the beach. They couldn't go swimming all week because the ocean was too cold. According to tomorrow's weather forecast, it's going to be hot and sunny. But Mr. and Mrs. Smith won't be able to go swimming tomorrow because they've got to leave early in the morning.

1. Mr. and Mrs. Smith couldn't go swimming on their vacation because . . .
2. The weather tomorrow is probably going to be . . .
3. Mr. and Mrs. Smith won't be able to go swimming tomorrow because . . .

HELEN'S ENGLISH EXAMINATION

Helen wasn't able to study for her English examination last night because she couldn't find her glasses. When she got to school this morning, she looked in her briefcase and her glasses were there. Unfortunately, it was too late. Helen didn't have any time to study in the morning, and she made a lot of mistakes on the examination. Poor Helen is very embarrassed.

4. Helen couldn't study for her examination because she lost her . . .
5. When did she find her glasses?
6. Helen is very embarrassed because . . .

Page 102 Exercise E

POOR BILL!

Poor Bill! He was driving over the State Street Bridge a few minutes ago when he got a flat tire. He tried to fix it by himself, but he couldn't, and he had to call a mechanic. Now he's really frustrated because he doesn't think he'll get to the airport on time.

1. Bill is . . .
2. While he was driving he . . .
3. He called . . .
4. He's probably going to be . . .
5. He might miss his . . .

Page 118 Exercise H

ON THE AIRPLANE

Good afternoon. This is Captain Harris speaking. Our plane will be leaving in just a few minutes. Soon we'll be flying over New York City, and you'll be able to see the baseball stadium on your right and Central Park on your left. We'll be flying over the Atlantic Ocean for three and a half hours. In a little while, you'll be having dinner, and after dinner you'll be seeing a movie. We'll be arriving in San Juan at 8:35. The weather in San Juan this evening is 70°F./21°C. and cloudy. It'll probably be raining when we get there.

IN THE HOSPITAL

Now Mr. Jones, after your operation, you'll probably be feeling weak for a few days. But don't worry! We'll be taking good care of you. Tomorrow you'll be staying in bed and resting comfortably all day. The nurses will be taking your pulse and blood pressure, and we'll be giving you a lot of soup and juice. The day after tomorrow you'll be walking and you'll be able to eat ice cream and yogurt. If everything is okay, you'll be leaving the hospital on Saturday. Do you have any questions?

YOU'LL FIND ME

When you come into the restaurant, you'll know who I am. I'll be wearing dark glasses and a raincoat. I'll be sitting by myself at a table in the corner, and I'll be drinking a glass of water and reading a newspaper. And I'll be looking for you. You'll find me. Don't worry!

Page 125 Exercise F

1. Did you have a good time at the school picnic last Saturday?
2. Was there anything good to eat?
3. How late did you stay?
4. Why did you leave so early?
5. Do you think next year's picnic will be better?

Page 132 Exercise D

ON THE BUS

Good morning. This is your bus driver, Jim Smith, speaking. I'm glad you'll be riding with us on this special weekend visit to New York City. We'll be leaving in just a few minutes and we'll be arriving in New York City at noon, in time for a delicious lunch at the Park Avenue Cafe. After lunch we'll be visiting the United Nations, and in the evening we'll be having dinner at one of New York's finest restaurants. Don't forget! You'll be staying at the Fifth Avenue Hotel across the street from the beautiful Museum of Modern Art. I'm sure you're all going to enjoy yourselves very much. If I can do anything to help you, please ask.

CORRELATION KEY

Student Text Pages	Activity Workbook Pages
Chapter 1	
2–3	1–6
4	7–8
5	9–10
Chapter 2	
10	11–12
11	13–15 (Exercises C, D, E)
12	15–17 (Exercises F, G)
13	18–21
Chapter 3	
18	22–23 (Exercise A)
19	23–25 (Exercises B, C, D)
21	26–28
22	29
Check-Up Test	30–31
Chapter 4	
26	32
27	33–35
29	36
30	37
31	38–40
Chapter 5	
36	41
37	42
39–40	43–48
42	49–51
43	52–53
Chapter 6	
46	54
47	55–57
49–50	58–61
Check-Up Test	62–63
Chapter 7	
56	64
57	65
58–59	66–68
60	69–70
63	71

Student Text Pages	Activity Workbook Pages
Chapter 8	
66	72–74
67	75–76
69	77–79
70	80
73	81
Check-Up Test	82–83
Chapter 9	
76	84–85 (Exercises A, B, C)
77	86–88 (Exercises D, E, F)
79	89 (Exercise G)
80–81	89–92 (Exercises H, I, J, K)
Chapter 10	
86	93–94
87	95
88	96–97 (Exercises D, E)
90–91	97–99 (Exercises F, G, H)
93	99–100 (Exercises I, J, K)
Check-Up Test	101–102
Chapter 11	
96–97	103–105
99	106–107
100–101	108
102	109–110
Chapter 12	
106	111
107–108	112–113
109	114–116
111–112	117–119
Chapter 13	
116	120–121 (Exercise A)
117	121–122 (Exercises B, C)
118–119	122–124 (Exercise D)
120	124–126 (Exercises E, F)
121–122	126–129 (Exercises G, H, I, J, K)
Check-Up Test	131–132

Note: A Correlation Key for this workbook may also be found in the Appendix of the *Side by Side* Core Conversation Course—Beginning Level.